PRE-FACES

Also by Jerome Rothenberg

Poems

White Sun Black Sun   (1960)
The Seven Hells of the Jigoku Zoshi (1962)
Sightings I-IX   (1964)
The Gorky Poems   (1966)
Between: Poems 1960–1963   (1967)
Conversations   (1968)
Poems 1964–1967   (1968)
Poems for the Game of Silence   (1971)
Poland/1931   (1974)
A Seneca Journal   (1978)
Vienna Blood   (1980)

Translations

New Young German Poets   (1959)
Hochhuth's "The Deputy," playing version   (1965)
Enzensberger's "Poems for People Who Don't Read Poems," with Michael
      Hamburger   (1968)
The Book of Hours & Constellations, or Gomringer by Rothenberg   (1968)
The 17 Horse Songs of Frank Mitchell X–XIII   (1970)

Anthologies

Ritual   (1966)
Technicians of the Sacred   (1968)
Shaking the Pumpkin   (1972)
America a Prophecy, with George Quasha   (1973)
Revolution of the Word   (1974)
A Big Jewish Book, with Harris Lenowitz and Charles Doria   (1977)

Recordings

From a Shaman's Notebook   (1968)
Origins & Meanings   (1968)
Horse Songs & Other Soundings   (1975)
6 Horse Songs for 4 Voices   (1978)
Jerome Rothenberg Reads Poland/1931   (1979)

Jerome Rothenberg
PRE-FACES
& Other Writings

A New Directions Book

ACKNOWLEDGMENTS

Grateful acknowledgment is made to the editors and publishers of the following journals and magazines in which some of the material in this volume previously appeared: *Alcheringa, I'kon, Kulchur, L=A=N=G=U=A=G=E, New Wilderness Letter, San Diego Magazine, Some/thing, Stony Brook.*

For acknowledgments of the first publication of some of the material in this volume, see page 228.

Manufactured in the United States of America
First published clothbound and as New Directions Paperbook 511 in 1981
Published simultaneously in Canada by George J. McLeod, Ltd., Toronto

Library of Congress Cataloging in Publication Data

Rothenberg, Jerome, 1931–
    Pre-faces & other writings.
    (A New Directions Book)
    Bibliography: p. 225
    Includes index.
    1. Poetry—Addresses, essays, lectures. I. Title.
PN1064.R66   1981   809.1   80–24031
ISBN 0–8112–0785–4
ISBN 0–8112–0786–2 (pbk.)

New Directions books are published for James Laughlin
by New Directions Publishing Corporation
80 Eighth Avenue, New York 10011

CONTENTS

Pre-Face to *Pre-Faces*   3

1 /DIALOGUING: AN OVER-VIEW
   From "A Dialogue on Oral Poetry," with William
     Spanos   9

2 /PRE-FACES & MANIFESTOS
   A Personal Manifesto   51
   From "Deep Image & Mode: An Exchange with Robert
     Creeley"   52
   Revolutionary Propositions   65
   Pre-Face I: *Technicians of the Sacred*   69
   Total Translation: An Experiment in the Presentation
     of American Indian Poetry   76
   Pre-Face II: *Shaking the Pumpkin*   93
   Pre-Face III: *Revolution of the Word*   99
   Pre-Face IV: *Origins*   112
   Pre-Face V: *A Big Jewish Book*   118
   From "Pre-Face to a Symposium on Ethnopoetics"   129

3 /POETICS
   On Anthologies   139
   From *Technicians of the Sacred*   144
     The Poetics of Sound   144
     Namings   145
     Images   146
     Bantu Combinations   148
     Aztec Definitions   149
     Praise Poems/Assemblages   151
     The Poetics of Chance (I): "The Book of
       Changes"   152
     The Poetics of Chance (II):
       "The Praises of the Falls"   154
   The Poetry of Number   156
   Gematria   158

Abraham Abulafia   160
At the Boundaries   162
Sounding Events   163
New Models, New Visions:
    Some Notes Toward a Poetics of Performance   165

4/BEYOND POETICS
Academic Proposal   175
Indians & Wilderness   176
The Poetics of Shamanism   186
God's Sexuality   190
America as a Woman   192
Offering Flowers   194
Tree Spirit Events   196
Gift Event   197
The Ghost Dance   198
Jesus   200
The Night Chant   202
Kunapipi   205
The Raingod Drama   208
Rain Event One   211
Old Man Coyote   212
Crazy Dog Events   214

5/THWARTING ENDS: A POST-FACE
The Thwarting of Ends: An Interview   219

Bibliography   225

Acknowledgments   228

Index   229

PRE-FACE TO PRE-FACES

Poets shape their worlds through their poems—& that might in itself seem sufficient means. But the world we share, & our interplay with it, calls again & again for *discourse:* in the case of poets, the setting forth of a poetics. I have found myself involved with that also, at first tentatively & then, once into it, discovering ways suited to my own temperament & to the sense I have (& that I find repeated insistently in going through these pages) that the discourse, like the poetry, must in all events resist rigidity & closure. At the same time—make no mistake about it—I've attempted, like other poets so engaged, to create a new & coherent poetics for our time.

Along with many of my generation, I've had a strong recoil from "literature" & "criticism" as a sufficient context for poetry. Criticism, I'd have to insist, is something different from the talk of poets & artists, & such talk about poetry & life—coming generously from my contemporaries—has fed me from the start of my own work. From my end I've tried to return their generosity by a kind of exploration that at a certain point seemed possible for me to do & possible to share with others. The main activity of my poetics has involved such acts of presentation: assemblage & performance & translation. I found early along that magazines were a natural vehicle for me, & that the magazines I edited inevitably expanded toward anthology. (I was already calling the third issue of my first magazine, *Poems from the Floating World,* an "ongoing anthology.")

About fifteen years ago I was encouraged to develop this anthology activity—along with a passion I already had for oral/tribal poetry & ritual—into the assemblage called *Technicians of the Sacred.* (I also found, in the aftermath, that there were many besides poets ready to follow the discourse behind that work.) The heart of the anthology was the poetry itself: the language works drawn from a range of human cultures. Accompanying those works, as a try at indicating their original context & their resemblance or lack thereof to the work of my contemporaries, was a series of commentaries & appendices (typical paraphernalia of scholarly anthologies, which I could here bend to my uses). And introducing all of it, a kind of work that I preferred to write out as PRE-FACE: the face or mask of the assembler/dissembler that sets out his intentions in the work.

I see all my work in this regard as a pre-face to something that comes after. If there's still any sense in talking of an avant-garde, then that must be it for me: an insistence that the work deny itself the last word, because the consequences of closure & closed mind have been & continue to be horrendous in the world we know. At any rate, each assemblage/anthology had a pre-face, & each set out to change & (usually) expand some aspect of the poet's territory: a second insistence, then, that runs through the present collection, that we must no longer think in terms of a single "great tradition" but can open to the possibility of getting at the widest range of human experience. And a third insistence closely following: that poetry & life aren't separate (whatever that might mean) but that the poetic discourse is a discourse, always, on the life from which the poem springs.

The present book is intended to show the continuities of my own poetics—a process that may be missed from reading single works & sections from those works in isolation. I've organized it as an anthology of my writings on poetry & related matters (essays, interviews, letters, event pieces, free-wheeling commentaries on specific texts, etc.); & I've set it up—toward some clarity, I hope—in five parts. It begins & ends with interviews: the first a written dialogue between myself & William Spanos, the last a discussion for a popular magazine in which the interviewer led me into a wider discussion of where we may be moving in the closing decades of this century. The second section ("Pre-Faces & Manifestos") involves a number of basic polemical/argumentative pieces, going back to my earliest (superceded but surviving) involvement with the imaging potential of language, & incorporating the various anthology pre-faces that give this book its title. In the third section ("Poetics"), I take up the line that I was developing from oral/tribal & avant-garde models in *Technicians of the Sacred,* & I follow it through my later writings, with emphasis also on what I came to call "the poetics of performance." (Like most of my writings in this vein, the basic procedure is by example.) And because poetry (& tribal poetry in particular) isn't isolated from other human experience, I use a fourth section ("Beyond Poetics") to show some of the ways in which traditional poetic & performance modes have entered the lives of those who engage in them.

For the rest, I hope that the writings themselves will make my intentions clear. Those intentions have included a desire to be forceful with "my own" concerns while not imposing them on others: a stance, if it works, that may be useful at a time when even poets—who should know better—seem nostalgic for authority & anxious about the freedom asserted in their own wild acts. That kind of thing would take a whole other book to discuss, but maybe the outline is already present in what follows.

Jerome Rothenberg
Encinitas, California
June 1, 1980

1 / Dialoguing: An Over-View

We're neither the first poets nor will we be the last.

From A DIALOGUE ON ORAL POETRY, with William Spanos (1975)

[*The following was designed as a "dialogue"—in written form —on what Spanos called the "oral impulse in contemporary American poetry." The resulting range, let me stress, was much wider than that stated in the title & gave me a chance to pull together & make explicit a number of concerns that had driven my work over the previous twenty years. Since we were following an interview structure, Spanos was in the position of questioner, & my strategy in responding was to avoid getting trapped in the vocabulary of "post-modern" criticism. If that was the game at hand, it allowed (like other games poets play) a chance to move at **unexpected angles** & to explore an actual poetics from previously **unexplored perspectives**. My first move in the interview was to **counter the assumption** of an exclusionary commitment to orality.*]

Spanos: The contemporary German philosopher Martin Heidegger keeps insisting that the fatal mistake of Western civilization was made when the post-Socratic philosophers translated the word *Logos* in the sentence "Man is the animal who has *Logos*" to mean "reason" or "judgment." This metamorphosis, he says, concealed the word's primordial meaning as "talk" or, rather, "oral speech" (*Rede*). And as a result the West eventually built up a civilization on the foundations of a coercive propositional language, a language of assertion, that in seeking to "take hold of," to master, the world, has ended up alienating "civilized" man from Being, the sacredness of existence, that it is only in the power of human speech to disclose. As I see it, one of the fundamental defining characteristics of contemporary literature, especially of contemporary American poetry, is a similar reaction against *Logos* as the rational Word or Final Cause—as the Omega, so to speak— in favor of an effort to dis-cover and recall the *Logos* as human speech which the West has covered over and forgotten. So, for example, Charles Olson, who has made Keats's Negative Capability a governing principle of his poetics, says in his seminal essay "Human Universe" that:

> We have lived long in a generalizing time, at least since 450 B.C. And it has had its effects on the best of men, on the best of things. Logos, or discourse, for example, has, in that time, so worked its abstractions into our concept and use of language that language's other function, speech, seems so in need of restoration that several of us go back to hieroglyphics or to ideograms to right the balance. (The distinction here is between language as the act of the instant and language as the act of thought about the instant.)

I'd like to begin, or, rather, to open up our "conversation" by asking if you think the effort to recover the oral impulse is a central and determining concern of contemporary American poets, and, if so, how you would interpret the motives informing this effort.

ROTHENBERG: I'm glad that you stressed the *you* in that question, which immediately personalizes it & allows for a more positive response. But let me start anyway with some qualifications about the word "oral" & whatever it is that we take to be its opposite. I think you present some usable terms in your statement, & I'm glad too that you avoid contrasting it with "written." But others don't, & it seems to me that the idea of writing is kicking around somewhere in the background & making for a good deal of confusion about the issues involved.

Speaking for myself, then, I would like to desanctify & demystify the written word, because I think the danger of frozen thought, of authoritarian thought, has been closely tied in with it. I don't have any use for "the sacred" in that sense— for the idea of book or text as the authoritative, coercive version of some absolute truth, changeless because written down & visible. That isn't to say that our problems with what Blake called "single vision" begin with writing, or to push for a tactical illiteracy by way of solution. Mr. Nixon or any man in power will be as dishonest verbatim as from written notes,

& when the argument reduces itself to that, it becomes a triviality or worse: another kind of authoritarianism in so far as it coerces poets or others to give up any skill, any means whatsoever. I don't think that writing is the ultimate cause of our troubles, but that writing itself comes about in response to a more fundamental change in human organization: a need to institutionalize laws, to control change & the uncertain acts of the individual, in the name of a tribe, of a class, of a nation, of a god, whatever. I'm not social scientist enough to dwell on this, but I want at least to acknowledge the wider picture—not to find a McLuhanesque scapegoat for civilized dilemmas—or if one is going to do that, to recognize the electronic media as similar threats to the idea of the oral.

But I've never thought of "oral" in this sense as my personal shibboleth, & I probably use it much less than you suppose. Because I happen to *write*—as do the other "oral poets" you mention elsewhere—& I'm not going to undo that. I'm much more honest as a writer than as a speaker, although one going view of *the* oral seems to equate it with *the* truthful. (I'm writing this reply, for example, not speaking it, because I don't want my statements conditioned by our face-to-face interview or by my own awkwardness: a combination that doesn't do much for my love of the truth.) And in part—the simplest part—my attitude toward "oral" poetry has nothing to do with my criticism of literature & the written word, etc. It is only that I'm responding to a conventional & deeply entrenched view of poetry that excludes or minimizes the oral; & I'm saying that the domain of poetry includes both oral & written forms, that poetry goes back to a pre-literate situation & would survive a post-literate situation, that human speech is a near-endless source of poetic forms, that there has *always* been more oral than written poetry, & that we can no longer pretend to a knowledge of poetry if we deny its oral dimension. All of which seems obvious to me, & yet when I do a book like *Technicians* or *Shaking the Pumpkin,* it still seems to flush out those who can't see or hear beyond the written word or printed page.

In that sense—of an oral medium prior to the written—I

think we're using the word as it turns up in ordinary discourse. But you're into much more in the question, touching on what for me are fundamental issues of poetry & reality: what we know & say, & how we say & know it. For this the contrast isn't "oral & literate" (written) but "oral & literal," where by literal I mean what you, or Heidegger, present as a kind of closed *Logos, Final Cause,* coercive propositional language, mastering the world rather than participating in it. Obviously the concern here isn't with a refinement of style, although as poets we may have some difficulties in disengaging ourselves from an old-fashioned literary context. That context itself may be part of the trap of categorical thinking, & it's certainly under attack now from a number of different directions. So I can as easily expect to find allies among scientists & linguists & other generally turned-on people as among those specifically engaged in the business of literature. (Notice that Olson, as a poet, isn't talking about poetry—isn't calling it "poetry"—but about language & discourse & speech, which is usefully the way we should be talking.)

Now if I try to get at some common idea that poets—the poets I still read—have particularly been into, I might start with a fairly open, ostensibly "irrational" proposition about the communication of the unverifiable: of an experience deliberately mediated by the *I,* therefore truly an experience. It seems to me that when the domain of discourse got split up, the poets ended up on that side, in the conflict between poetry & philosophy/shamanism & theology/individual & state/oral & literal that Plato first called to our attention. (They didn't all stay there, but that's a different matter.) More recently it's become clear that it isn't a bad place to be & that the scientists (who picked up from the philosophers after the literal theologians had caved in) may be edging toward a reconciliation. But where earlier scientific language had attempted to evade the individual experience, poetry was becoming radically empirical & phenomenological. From Blake & Whitman on, modern poetry has assumed an accumulation of selves—of poets writing out of their own experience—that will together make up a total image of the world. It has gradually abandoned generality (including the subjective lyrical kind), while going as doggedly after its objects as science after its. But its particulars are the particulars of *this* immediate experience, & (or because) the experiencing "self" is itself in a continuous process of change.

Let me take the "Objectivists" as an example, since their name, their official tag, might seem to contradict what I was saying about the mediating *I*. But Zukofsky is clearly pointing to a dialectic, derived from a metaphor of "vision," in which the poet's "clear physical eye" (pronounced *I*) must be the instrument which brings the "rays of the object . . . to a focus"/ "thinking with the things as they exist," etc.—or what Oppen gets into a very neat phrase: that the "virtue of the mind is that emotion which causes to see." In other words, the return to the object also implies a "seer"—an *I* through which subject & object are joined—as in Rimbaud's earlier formulation or the even more distant Copper Eskimo name for a shaman: "the one who has eyes." [See below, pages 105, 186.]

It took me a long time to see the value of the "Objectivist" strategy in relation to "vision"—the getting rid, as Olson described it, "of the lyrical interference of the individual as ego, of the 'subject' and his soul, that peculiar presumption by which western man has interposed himself between what he is as a creature of nature (with certain instructions to carry out) and those other creations of nature which we may, with no derogation, call objects." But none of this denies a "seer" so much as it refocuses our attention on the object of sight—its purpose & the process by which it occurs. So, taking it a step further back & connecting it to that change from "literal" to "oral," Buckminster Fuller wrote:

Heisenberg said that observation alters the phenomenon observed. T. S. Eliot said that studying history alters history. Ezra Pound said that thinking in general alters what is thought about. Pound's formulation is the most general, and I think it's the earliest.

And in that "most general" formulation, I find a connection (as Pound would probably not have) to that equally important strategy once hammered home by Breton & the Surrealists, in which the dream vision was brought into waking life; or even (& still in pursuit of the "vision") to the Dadaists' "discovery" that chance & accident could themselves create poems & structures which in turn became the thing seen ("free of lyrical interference," etc.), but following the work of art rather than before it.

Except for that last view, I've been limiting myself here to concepts of vision & thought, which can presumably exist without a construct or a visible performance. But clearly all these poets—Surrealists & "Objectivists," etc.—were construct-oriented, language-oriented people. That would be the principal distinction between the visionary & the poet, the contemplative thinker & the artist—what the "Objectivists" got at in the second reading of their name, the idea of the poem-as-object: "a big or little machine made of words" (W. C. Williams). Of the early American modernists, Williams remains the most convincing in his stress on the structural & linguistic side of the "oral vs. literal" proposition:

> The mutability of the truth. Ibsen said it. Jefferson said it. We should have a revolution of some sort in America every ten years. The truth has to be redressed, re-examined, re-affirmed in the new mode. There has to be new poetry. But the thing is that the change, the greater material, the altered structure of the inevitable revolution must be *in* the poem, in it. Made of it. It must shine in the structural body of it.

So, just as the (modern) poem derives from a particular vision (an experience deliberately mediated by the *I*), it takes shape in a particular structure & a particular language, with the *I* again at center. And there is again, or there should be, no recourse to higher authority—neither to a coercive closed vision, nor to a coercive closed form, nor to a coercive poetic vocabulary or syntax—but instead the poem emerges from the linguistic particulars of *this* experiencing self. At least I would see that as the second consequence of that "most general formulation," which Fuller credited to Pound & which in some form or other (automatic writing, *free* verse, organic form, etc.) was shared by most of those early modernists who had begun to sense the consequences of their break with literal thinking. The idea of the oral—of a source of forms renewed in each instance—remains germinal; so important in the end that some of us have come to see it as concurrent with, or prior to, that other ("visionary") business of the poem. And the way you've set it up in the question, it would now seem to cover whatever other anti-literal approaches—chance operations, say, or concrete poetry—develop the idea of each poem as a separate structural & cognitive instance. In which case the poem becomes the field of the poet's action, & as he opens up that field, his action becomes coterminous with that of anyone who recognizes his own immediate relation to the world & speaks it.

In fulfillment of Blake's prophecy: "Would that all God's people were poets!"

SPANOS: Your response is provocative all along the way. But it's your definition of the poets that interest you in terms of the "I" which is also "eye" (an equation that Olson too seems to make, especially in Letter 6 of the *Maximus Poems*: "polis is/eyes . . .") that I find especially interesting. I notice from this point on a gradual but rather definite and perhaps definitive shift from the oral to a visual context, from the metaphor of voice to the "metaphor of 'vision,' " from the notion of poet as speaker to poet as "see-er" or, to pin down what really whets my interest, "seer." I'd like to pick up on this movement later on, but for now let me take my *first* question a little farther.

Your deep interest in the oral ritual expression of "archaic" and tribal peoples, especially of the American Indian, is, of course, reflected in the "ethnopoetics" of your anthologies, and of *Alcheringa*, the journal you co-edit with Dennis Tedlock. This interest clearly suggests to me your personal commitment to the task of recovering the—or *an*—oral tradition on behalf of the renewal of American poetry—and, I take it, of modern Western man. What, in your view, has the "primitive" or tribal oral tradition to offer contemporary American poetry in particular?

ROTHENBERG: First off it raises the idea of "oral tradition" itself (no matter whether *the* or *an*) & its compatibility with, centrality to, whatever schemata of a "poetry of changes" we've developed among ourselves. I'll get around to "primitive" & "tribal" shortly, but for the moment a perfectly good formulation (of the two terms "oral" & "tradition") comes, say, in Gershom Scholem's, "Revelation & Tradition as Religious Categories," where he's talking about the survival, in an otherwise "literal" context, of the Jewish "oral law" as process or kabbalah:

> Tradition, according to its mystical sense, is Oral Torah, precisely because every stabilization in the text would hinder and destroy the infinitely moving, the constantly progressing and unfolding element within it, which would otherwise become petrified. The writing down and codification of the Oral Torah, undertaken in order to save it from being forgotten, was therefore as much a protective as (in the deeper sense) a pernicious act.

In that sense, the persistence of the question among the Jews— Jews who take themselves seriously as the supreme people-of-the-book—indicates to me how deep the whole subterranean culture, the tribal-&-oral, can run, has run in fact in all our histories. And for ourselves, now, for those of us who think of poetry as linked to, as that very process of unfolding & changing, let me venture a guess that what we're recovering is *the* oral tradition (the idea of that *per se*), but what we're creating is *an* oral tradition—& that we'll get to the first only by shooting for the second.

Over all, however, I would want to expand the context of recovery: not to isolate it but to see it as part of a greater enterprise: a greater scheme or strategy described by Duncan out of Whitman as the composition of an all-inclusive "symposium of the whole." [See below, page 119.] This, it seems to me, is a terrific paradigm of what's possible to us today: what we've come to by a number of different roads: as poets (if that's the right word) or simply as people to whom many awarenesses are now present. If so, then the history of the West (that particular niche of so-called civilization) has come to a point of possible qualitative change . . . or the great subculture surfacing at last. Because it seems to me that for 2,000 years at least (or, more accurately, 5,000) the impulse of "civilization" has been to supercede & annihilate its past: to remove from our psyches & flesh, therefore from our institutions as well, the "*old* man" (& certainly the woman, animal, etc.). Religion & science, as we woke up as kids to find them, are both very militant, very absolute philosophies in that regard: tough & progressivistic in favor of the "new man" & "dying to the past": transforming that old savage/adam nature so as to get us full-clothed & scrubbed before return to paradise. Obviously they haven't utterly succeeded but been plagued by heresies & intellectual eccentrics—which failure acts finally to keep the options open: an option that the "romantics" seized to start a reconsideration of the total human experience, the total biological experience as well. Science— paradoxically perhaps, & here's the clincher—begins the reconsideration of human continuities, & really good science supplies the information about ourselves as a species & part of a biological continuum, etc., that the poets will then transform from the idea of something to be superceded to the idea of something to be accepted & extended. (But carefully, let me tread carefully at this point, so not to demand in turn the obliteration of all that's accrued over the intervening years, pushing a new literalism—in the name of the tribal sub-cult & so on—but willing to stand with Blake's continuous desystematization, or Whitman's contradictions, Olson's "will to change," or Duchamp's "I have forced myself to contradict myself," etc.: those modernist proposals for a present poetry of changes.)

So I don't see, to get back to your question, that it's a matter of a return to the primitive, but a recognition of the primitive, the source of what we are, as a necessary part of the human inheritance, both because it very simply is that (& we deny its present existence, in us, at our peril) & because it has something (some things) to offer now. Therefore, in outline:

—the traditions in question add to any reconsideration of poetry as "vision" & "communion" a series of authentic instances (historical & cultural) in which such functions were realized;

—they provide the idea of the oral & mythic as self-corrective tellings, & the evidence of how it works;

—they give a functional dimension to "meaning" or "significance" in the poetic act: the evidence that even apparently minimal forms may have a great complexity of function ("the smallest things can turn you on"—P. Blackburn), & that without the kabbalists' *kavvanah* (i.e., intention), the weightiest expression can be the most trivial, etc.—but at the same time, an expanded notion of alternative poetic & linguistic structures;

—they point to the existence of what Gary Snyder calls "models of basic nature-related cultures": this at the beginning of what may be a post-technological age (post-modern, let me say, in the only sense that term has meaning for me), in which we may have to recover certain basic human tools without reliance on unavailable sources of energy (or: what happens to the light show when the lights go out; how much sound can you generate without Con Ed, etc.?): toward a fusion of ecology & poetics;

—they lead to a recognition that cultures, like species, are irreplaceable once extinct: the product of millennia;

—in the Amerindian instance, etc., they afford a means of enlarging our experience of the continent—in time & space;

—they comprise a necessary body of knowledge at a time when "the wave of the future would seem to be the growing awareness of Europeans that they are themselves on the other side of the frontier of developing and expanding people . . . (when) we are being told (and a few are listening) that Europe is brutal and brilliant, successful—and dead . . ." (thus the anthropologist, Paul Bohannan: 1966).

And for all of this, the term "primitive"—except for the useful dichotomy with "civilized" that thinkers like Stanley Diamond still would stress—is not only a debased coinage, a block to our consideration of our total needs, but hides the truth it should most helpfully make clear: that the models in question don't so much bind us to the past, as (in words Gary Snyder once wrote me) ease our entry to the future. [See below, page 189.]

SPANOS: Despite the beautiful and almost persuasive way you commit your ethnopoetics to the future in your last remarks, I'm still a little uneasy about your account of the "greater enterprise," as you call it, especially about what I see as a tendency to minimize man's historicity. On both the cultural level and the level of literary history, what you say seems to me—I may be exaggerating—to emphasize universals, organic, to be sure, but universals nonetheless—inclusive/timeless paradigms or models (myths)—at the expense of historical differentiation. Historicity loses its priority to form, tends to get absorbed, in other words, into a timeless structural whole in which change is, in fact, extension from a fixed and stable center. You seem to be aware of this danger in the parenthetical warning to yourself against the possibility of "pushing a new literalism—in the name of the tribal sub-cult & so on."

But, again, I'd like to postpone this crucial issue until later on when we can confront it directly. For the time being, I'd like to pursue the thrust of my question about the potential contribution of the archaic oral tradition to contemporary American poetry. In a well-known passage from *Paterson* (II), Williams says:

> unless there is
> a new mind there cannot be a new
> line, the old will go on repeating
> itself with recurring deadliness . . .

What you've emphasized so far in your response is the kind of contribution the "oral" tradition can make to the contemporary consciousness, to the achievement of the "new mind." Can you be more specific about its potential contributions to the formal character of American poetry? What kind of "line," in other words, does the "new mind" you envisage imply?

ROTHENBERG: Of all the formal characteristics of the new American poetry, the line is probably the most language specific, conditioned at only second or third hand by what we know outside the language. The paradigm, set by such as Whitman, Williams, Stein, & so on, probably still holds, unless the pattern in Cage's lectures or Antin's talking poems—

or the work of Bernadette Mayer & other, even younger poets I know who work outside all verse conventions—is a true paradigmatic departure. Yet even here I'm mindful that someone like Dennis Tedlock, say, shows the possibility of translating from an oral tradition precisely those turnings in spoken narrative that follow from the model of open verse in English. What's more, his insight into that has not only been influenced by American open-verse practice but has then come to influence the way that Antin, e.g., sees talking as essentially "poetic" in its movement.

Aside from line, though, the possibility of formal influences isn't at all limited or ambiguous, but involves all those analogies between "modern" & "primitive" forms that I've tried to show in *Technicians* & *Shaking the Pumpkin*. (I'm still leaving open the question of whether the "primitive" is influencing the "modern" or the "modern" is directing our attention to forms we may now recognize as poems in tribal/oral cultures. Most probably it goes both ways.) Repetition patterns—the nearly universal practice of redundant utterance, or what Antin calls "phrasal poetry" in his discussion of the "prose" work of Gertrude Stein—would be the most obvious example of a shared formal process that emerges in the move toward a new "orality." That kind of influence or re-enforcement can come not only through translations but from oral modes in English, like the phrase & intonation patterns out of blues, which have had an obvious & *direct* impact on most of the new Black poets, as well as any number of White ones from the '60s on. (And here, in interchange between two forms of "English," the *line* itself comes into play!)

I don't want to go over too much old ground, so let me just tick off a few key concepts, & for the rest refer you back to the Pre-Faces & the Books of "Events" & "Extensions" in *Technicians* & *Pumpkin*. It seems to me that since the 1950s (in some ways for several decades before), we have been working increasingly with a performance model of the poem, for which the written versions serve as the notation or the score. Forms of performance such as "sound poetry" obviously can be related back to the wordless poems/songs of the older tribal cultures, & contemporary sound poets have clearly been aware of this from the Futurists & Dadaists on. In my own work (I'm thinking particularly of the "Horse Songs") I've used translation as a process for the composition of mixed forms (words & "pure"-sound) based on mixed forms in the Navajo, & there the influence of the tribal/oral is clearly one to one. [See below, page 85.] (But remember here that Mac Low or that Cage in his *Mureau* pieces, & so on, have themselves created mixed forms in the normal, head-on manner of the avant-garde inventor.) Redundancy & repetition would again come into the performance area, to remind us that the poem isn't the single utterance, the synopsis, but the totality of the event —much as a musical composition like Satie's *Vexations* suggests a performance model akin to repetitive Plains Indian chanting or to the Hebrew "Alphabet Event" I give in *Poland/1931:*

(1)
Recite the 221 alphabets while walking in a circle.
Repeat the event 442 times.

(2)
Do the first Alphabet Event walking backwards.
Recite the alphabets starting from the end.

(I am here thinking also of the systematic language happenings—including systematic chance—that have been crucial to kabbalistic & oracular poetry throughout the ages.) The result of all of this is an alteration of our actual time sense: in these examples toward an extension of time, or in others (like the "Osage Simultaneities" in *Shaking the Pumpkin)* toward the kind of synchronous performance of which Mac Low, again, has been the principal advocate on our own terrain.

Poetry on some such model runs the range from the "stand-up" poet (the stance most common to our poetry "readings") to forms of intermedia as complex in their inclusions as traditional, tribal ritual-events in theirs. [See below, page 70.] Once we're into these, we learn as much from other art & artists (or from the experience, simply, of other human beings) as we do from poetry & poets—moving into a situation in which the boundaries begin to blur, as if to bring us back to a time before they were established. And it's for this reason—along with the energies, the sense of powers implied—that so many poets & artists have looked for both analogues & spurs to their own work in the tribal/oral cultures & in the subterranean, often "magical" traditions that have survived the ages of division, of separation into isolated modes.

SPANOS: I have noticed that in the "Pre-Face" (as you put it) to your influential anthology *America a Prophecy,* which is a sometimes persuasive manifesto announcing the new American poetic imagination, you don't make a clear distinction between an early and a late modernism. But there are rather glaring omissions in your references to modern and contemporary poets: T. S. Eliot, W. B. Yeats, W. H. Auden, John Crowe Ransom, Allen Tate, Randall Jarrell, Robert Lowell, for example. You also rather pointedly celebrate poets whom the early Moderns and their critical counterparts, the New Critics, held in suspicion and in some cases even disdain: I'm thinking, for example, of William Blake and especially of Walt Whitman. Does this mean that you do, in fact, distinguish between a Modern and a Postmodern American poetry? If so, why do you think early Modernism has run its course or arrived at a dead end? What in your opinion, in other words, are the essential limitations of the "classic" modern American poem?

ROTHENBERG: I find here that we're working on two very different sets of assumptions, so that I can't even start to answer without first giving my own sense of "modern" & "postmodern." The second of those terms has bothered me since I first heard about it—not among poets who talk about continuities but among academics who don't—& the question helps me understand why.

To begin with, in my own chronology of modern poetry (& for me "modern" means the recovery of that sense of "oral" or "non-literal" we were discussing earlier), that string of poets you reeled off is largely out of place. They're twentieth-century poets, most of them skillful & even intelligent, but working for the most part within very conventional limitations as to form & content—& with varying degrees of hostility to modern poetry. If we were talking about modern painting, you wouldn't throw Burchfield & Grant Wood at me & expect a serious discussion. And my point is that modernism in poetry has to be discussed at its extremes—just as it does in painting—otherwise you can't know if you've gotten past it. Now, by "early" modern poetry I'm talking about the term as it came into use around the First World War, not only in America & England but throughout the so-called Western world: a poetry of changes, experiment, destruction & creation, questioning old structures & inventing new ones, blurring fixed distinctions, opening the domain, & so on. I'm very grateful for all of that as a beginning, as a paradigm of poetics & creative work in the twentieth century; & what disturbs me about most of the poets you mention is that they raised an opposition that tried to halt the modernist ferment, to pull back to a conventional poetics somewhat modified by the modernist turn of events but fundamentally conservative in outlook: a familiar Anglo-Saxon & class-oriented view of language & high culture. I don't know if they ever used the term *post*-modern about themselves, but they could have (more easily than most of us, in fact), since what they asserted was that "modern poetry" (read: Eliot's Tudor verse style) had established itself, & that the next step was a return to standard metrics & a beefed-up "great tradition." It seems ridiculous in retrospect, but as late as the 1950s, Delmore Schwartz could describe all of that as a "poetic revolution" or a "revolution in poetic taste," which I would take, at least, as a contradiction in terms: a deception based on Eliot's criticism (literary & social), & on Pound's reluctance to follow through on the implications of his own poetic practice. [See below, page 100.] What Schwartz was defending, anyway, was a middle-ground strategy: a rear-guard response (by Eliot, Tate, & others) to the "anarchistic"thrust of modern poetry & art (free verse, free thought, free love, etc.), which shows up also in that "suspicion" or "disdain" of Blake & Whitman that you mention. It was with a clear awareness of this that Williams spoke of *The Waste Land* as "the great catastrophe to our letters," because he saw that beneath the cover of an actual structural innovation (as much Pound's as Eliot's) was an impulse to pull up stakes & get back to the narrow & comfortable limits of the inherited past.

Now, if there were only Eliot's criticism & that of the New Critics to define the "classic" modern poem, I would write off modernism as the dead end you mention. But, as I said, we must be talking about two different things to start with, & for me all that tasteful, middle-ground retrenchment is almost wholly opposed to what I would see as early modernism (Stein, Williams, Cummings, Pound, Duchamp, the Dadaists, Surrealists, Objectivists, & so on)—work that stands in a germinal relationship to the poetry that's been developed in my own generation. I'm aware of differences here too, though I don't need the prefix to define them—that the early modernists are more immediately concerned at some point in Tzara's "great negative work of destruction," or that they hold back conversely (the Americans, in particular) in fear of the consequences; that they affect a purity of stance that breaks them into warring camps with manifestos, -isms, & the rest; that they're elitist & defensive, uncertain of their roots & cultures; that they have the possibility & the "problem" of coming at new forms from nowhere (even in the act of breaking forms), so can't, like Olson in "Projective Verse," say, build from work already done, or, like Blackburn, acknowledge:

> We have had our gene-
> ration of innovators, 19
> 15 & the rest.
> What Pound and Williams & Moore have done
> is in the air, is, perhaps, the air.
> Let the species now give rise to a few
>   *masters*
>   (since the fields are open
>   and the air cleared)

—or, as someone might say of another set of innovators, the Dadaists had no "dadaists" before them.

So what has run its course—if I can get back to the language of your question—is the absurdity that filled the schools, etc., when I was growing up. The other I would hope has fulfilled itself in us through whatever continuity of intentions is possible in a poetics of change—so that we can work out our own awareness, function as poets in the sense I spoke about before: to allow the revolution to go on. But that's for the future to decide.

SPANOS: Yes, I think we're working on two somewhat different sets of assumptions about the definition of "modernism" (and it very well may be that mine derives from being a captive of the New Criticism during my student years, though I doubt if that's completely the case). But before addressing the issue—it's related to or rather it includes the questions about where your emphasis falls between oral and visual, timelessness and historicity—let me develop the immediate line of questioning a little bit more.

In reaction to nineteenth-century positivism and its Technological City—the "Crystal Palace," as Dostoyevsky calls it in *Notes from Underground*—the early moderns (I mean the Symbolists and Imagists) also searched for models outside the "Western" humanistic dispensation. They followed the lead of sculptors like Epstein, Gaudier-Brzeska, Brancusi, and painters like Picasso, Wyndham Lewis, Modigliani, and in the process "discovered" the art of Africa, ancient Egypt, and above all, the Orient: India, China, and Japan—and a way of breaking poetry out of the coercive linear time track of the Gutenberg Galaxy into a more "visionary" and "sacramental" mode. As a matter of fact, Mircea Eliade, one of the most important sources, I take it, of the renewed interest in the "primitive" imagination, has said in *Cosmos and History: The Myth of the Eternal Return* that the works of T. S. Eliot and James Joyce—and he certainly could have added Yeats and some of D. H. Lawrence—is "saturated with nostalgia for the myth of eternal repetition," which is at the heart of the non-historical, pre-literate tribal consciousness of primitive societies. How would you distinguish between, say, Eliot's and Yeats's sense of "primitivism" (I'm using the word not in resistance, but for lack of a better) and yours? Lawrence, like Pound, though

25

clearly for different reasons, seems to have survived the general reaction against early modernism. Where does he fit into your differentiation?

ROTHENBERG: This follows out of the same view of modernism as the previous question, so there's again a problem, in answering it directly, to make sure we're speaking about the same dichotomies & cast of characters, & so on. I don't, for example, see as fundamental a split as you do between the "modernists" & the nineteenth-century "positivists," when so many of the modernists I would name were in fact incorporating aspects of the technology into their own work. And certainly by the time it gets to my own generation (with its pick-up on pop culture & the machines that transmit it), we're at the very least primitivizing the media & choosing what still speaks to us in that "technological city." Anyway there are too many shadings here for me to simply agree that the earlier painters & sculptors you list, say, were all that "saturated with nostalgia" for tribal consciousness & myths (I hope you don't take the myths themselves as nostalgic)—& if you would consider some of the poets who were more truly the painters' equivalents than the "symbolists" or even the several big guns you mention, you'd see that that was the case with modern poetry as well. I mean, however it works out in any individual case, to count oneself into an "avant-garde" is to set up at least a little hedge against nostalgia. And the point, anyway, is that they weren't simply longing for the past, but were actively changing our idea of what the present & past are, both together. So I think it's poor judgment to think of those discoveries of "primitive" Africa, & so on, as mere "nostalgia": a condition I would take as more of a desire for the near or familiar past (the day before yesterday, so to speak), whereas here it's a recognition that the outlook of that day was too narrow to truly define & explore the multiple dimensions of the human that were then emerging. A Chinese poet may be nostalgic about Tu Fu: an American looking at Tu Fu's work can see the opening of possibilities other than those given by our culture. And this need to hold or incorporate diverse chronologies simultaneously ("non-linearly," if you want to use McLuhan) can produce as experimental a condition as that generated from our day-to-day experience—is in that sense not antiquarian but, as I understand the term, essentially "modern."

Now, most of that latter quality I find to be missing or badly compromised in Eliot's criticism, though the yearning for the near past is clearly very strong. It's this nostalgia & the accompanying despair about the other possibilities, both "primitive" & "modern," that endeared him to the middle-grounders: an essentially conservative position, pushing history or poetry back a little in the name of, let's say, "law & order." So what Lawrence & Pound "survive" isn't the reaction to modernism but to the attentuation of modernism: the resort to "church" & "monarchy" & "picking up the meters." Their relation to the past—even if I don't find it as serviceable, say, as that of the Surrealists—at least maintains a sense of continuum with the "pagan" & the "primitive," rather than with the genocidal institutions that sought to wipe them out.

Lawrence was very much into the new verse, but even more so, the "reactionary" side of the change in consciousness—all that "primitive" & erotic energy he postulated & wanted, though he was probably as terrified of it (with a thoroughly Anglo-Saxon, racial fear) as Eliot. And at the same time he was put off by almost every other aspect of the "technological city," with the kind of aesthetic disgust you run across in turn-of-the-century "decadents" & Symbolists—much more there than with the typical early modernists from, say, the 20s on. Pound's paganism, in that sense, was a prettier, clearly more literary proposition, closer to Eliot's classicism, I suppose, though the drift of his politics was more extreme & dangerous, getting himself bogged down in the Renaissance & so on, then with Fascism & the perpetuation of the nation-state. But think of what he contributes even so: the collage composition of the *Cantos,* the pivotal breakthroughs in translation, the sense of history as vortex, the transmission of an actual alternative tradition.

In my own generation, as contrasted to Lawrence more than to many other modernists, the anti-technological side is muted, although the dangers of technology are now more clear. We don't on the whole insist on a pure "primitivism," a death of the machine, say, unless the conditions naturally arise: & having grown up with motors & electronic media, we aren't against them from aesthetic disgust or nostalgia but on ecological grounds. In that way, then, a composer like Pauline Oliveros can fluctuate between electronic performances & something as rudimentary as banging rocks together. And even Gary Snyder drives a car & rides in airplanes.

But all of that can change of course—may be out of our control even now & pulling us toward some kind of truly post-technological situation. In which case the *pure* primitivists will turn out to have had the greater insight. Anyway, I don't find that in conflict with the "modernism" of my generation: just a more extreme fulfillment of the critique of civilization: the "primitive" side of the vision.

SPANOS: Since contemporary American poets of your general persuasion—Charles Olson, Robert Creeley, Allen Ginsberg, Gary Snyder, Robert Duncan, David Antin, for example (I could have named a dozen more)—have been reacting against the "school" of Eliot, they must also be reacting against the *Tradition* as Eliot, his contemporaries, and the New Critics in the English and American universities canonized it. I mean, of course, the tradition which makes irony and paradox the essential characteristics of the greatest poetry and which goes back from Eliot through Laforgue and Baudelaire to Donne and the Metaphysical poets, Dante, etc. What, then—to bring what you've been saying into clear focus—is the *tradition* as you and your generation see it (including the key contemporary figures—ideologues as well as poets)?

ROTHENBERG: I'll break this into a couple of stages: first give as general a statement as I can about the characteristics of poetry (whether "great" or not) that interests me, & then fill in some names & works, both contemporary & ancient.

The most sweeping generalization in *America a Prophecy* spoke of a "tradition (or poetry) of changes"—a term I prefer to Quasha's "metapoetics," with its echo of metaphysical & so on. I think of that not only as a "modern" strategy but as underlying the poetic process back to its beginnings: the root idea of metamorphosis & the poet's freedom to reconsider & review the common sources. In our time especially, when our knowledge of the past (in fact & dream) is constantly expanding, it would be selling ourselves cheap to slip back into an idolatrization of the sources as fixed or the "tradition" as absolute & static. So, by contrast to the "literal" view that repeats the past by rote, the alternative tradition makes-it-new at every step—& in this sense "tradition" & "experiment" or "change" come very naturally together. But that much should be obvious from my remarks about the "oral" earlier along.

It should be obvious too that in a poetry that accepts contradictions, irony & paradox aren't just the marks of a "superior" literary style but very human, very natural responses. And that may be one reason why I've turned to the so-called "primitive" more than to the kind of "Eastern" view that annihilates the contradictions—why I find in tribal narrative & vision that realism & "principle of ambivalence" which Stanley Diamond tells us are "incorporated into the myths and rituals of primitive peoples to an extraordinary degree . . . and most directly realized in the figure of the trickster." This isn't irony as something devious or clever, but at the very heart of things: as part of a continuum, another aspect of that *direct* treatment of event or object as immediate (unmediated) image that the analytic critics couldn't deal with, but had to interpose their own interpretations into prose. Dante, of the poets you mention, seems incredibly direct in that sense. And even a "metaphysical" like Donne is interesting or exciting because of what he *first* presents: the numinous in physical assault upon the body; lovers becoming compasses; the moon producing tides & tears; stage-sets with lights & shadows; eyes that flash *real* pictures; angels who appear in flames & voices. If a poet doesn't have that from the start, then irony & paradox won't pull it out for him.

So as I go along, I'm more & more for taking poets' statements as given—as a way to transform my own sense of space & time—in contrast to which "irony" (as literary device that works like "symbolism," by indirection) would seem to function like a kind of dodge. In that sense the class of unimaged metaphor, of which "my love is a rose" is a pretty but trivial example, gives way in my mind to Gertrude Stein's insistence that a rose is a rose is a rose: "that in that line the rose is red for the first time in English poetry for a hundred years." But when Dante comes at his great image of the rose at the end of *Paradiso,* that's different: not because he's talking about God & Burns about a lady (ladies do mean more to me than God), but because of the *envisioning* that's taking place there. Or again, when the Cuna Indian shaman "enters" the body of his patient & travels her womb in search of the animals & the Lilith-like goddess who have prevented childbirth, one recognizes the condition described in Lévi-Strauss's quote or paraphrase from Rimbaud: that "metaphor can change the world." [See below, page 120.]

It's such occasions that I've tried to explore or draw from—in the same sense, I think, in which one speaks of a "tradition." If we're going to adapt the word to where we are (some would suggest just dropping it), we can't restrict it to a monolineal inheritance, but have to use it in a new sense as "discovery" or "map": a mapping of those times & places, simply those works in which envisioning occurred. These can include the "Western" classics as presumably familiar ground, but should in no sense be taken as culminating in them. And the beginnings would be as far back as we can see them, which in the "West" would get us to Lascaux or to that glimpse of language Marshack teaches us to read from marks on bone:

Moon of the Thaw
Moon of the Spring Salmon Run
Moon of the Calving
Moon of the Flowers
Moon of the Moulting
Moon of the Rutting Bison
Moon of the Nut
Moon of the First Fruit

—those "Upper Paleolithic notations" which, in their relation to "Siberian and American Indian traditions," bring us back to something universal maybe: the last truly intercontinental culture until our own.

This is the source of that *"mainstream* of poetry that goes back to the old tribes & has been carried forward by the great subterranean culture" *—the* tradition if I were finally to name it. In ancient Europe & the Mediterranean (three continents included in that one), we've by now unearthed a range of poetries that include Sumerian, Egyptian, Babylonian, Hittite, & so on, along with those Greeks & Jews who once made up all of our known beginnings. If we can still relate to distant Homers & Isaiahs (both historically &, in Pound's sense, as "contemporaneous in the mind"), then it should be possible too to relate to the poetry of *Gilgamesh* & the *Enuma Elish*. And I don't see that this denies "history" (you would do better to confront the old-line academics on that one), but rather fulfills it—gives us a new opening through which we've discovered whole networks of connections & found that even the full accounts of Jew & Greek had been obscured for us. That much was Olson's insistence, as I understand it, & I've recently tried to get it down myself, writing the "pre-face" to Doria & Lenowitz's *Origins* [see below, page 112], in which I let myself sound awe-struck at the great mix & turmoil of those actual Near Eastern cosmogonies: whole cauldrons of images that don't (in our retrospective reading of them) wipe out conflict & contradiction but allow that "clash of symbols," which I there attribute to the French philosopher Ricoeur [page 117]. To which let me add (for the record) that it's this outlook, applied to similar materials, that makes poetry, as a faith, more central to me than religion—& why, while I understand the move to particular myths & mythic systems, I feel no urge to join it.

What holds for those other times & places carries into the "New" World as well. For years we've internalized (or so it almost seems) a sense of our traditions on this continent & of ourselves as makers & inheritors of a poetry in conflict with the accepted orders. From my own perspective (but shared,

---

* Masthead slogan for *Alcheringa* and *New Wilderness Letter.*

I think, with many others) I see the Indian *poesis* as our primary ground, including the great Meso-American poetries still preserved. I don't mean this as an accomplished fact of poetry & consciousness but as a possibility to be explored. And I don't see it either in a narrowly native context but again as part of that wider, still emerging "world" picture I've spoken of above. So while I would project the "Indian" as our base or widest ground, I would look also toward those later lines that come together in our works. Thus

: European poetries, with a particular stress on the numinous & mystical (both literary like Edward Taylor & self-developed, even "oral," like the Shakers), & that anti-puritanical thrust first mapped by Williams in *In the American Grain;*

: similar & often crucial "Eastern" lines (again both "literary" & "tantric");

: the new poets & transcendentalists of the nineteenth century, notably Emerson & Thoreau, Melville & Hawthorne (both in verse & in prose);

: the essential presence of Whitman & the emergence of isolated verse experimenters like Dickinson;

: the continuing input of European poets from Blake & the Romantics to Rimbaud & the Surrealists, & so on;

: & from the First World War on, the development of a continuous movement toward the exploration of consciousness, language, & poetic structure—what we can see & say & make.

This latter movement (which I've tried to reinterpret in *America a Prophecy* & *Revolution of the Word*) explodes *circa* 1914 in a series of transformative moves, then continues UNBROKEN to our own time.

That, anyway, is how I would start to construct a "tradition" alternative to Eliot's & appearing at its extremes (I see Blake & Milton, for example, as major European predecessors)

to be a nearly total reversal of values. Yet I think (without claiming more than my own particular & still limited perspective from the U.S.A.) that it's truer to our actual circumstances than the Leavis-like "great" tradition you outlined in your question—& a lot more complex in its interweavings. So, if you'd like me to take off on your wording in that synopsis of Eliot & Leavis, to put it in a nutshell, I would say that I'm speaking of THE TRADITION WHICH TAKES VISION & CONFLICT AS THE ESSENTIAL CHARACTERISTICS OF POETRY; SEES THESE AS BOUND TO THE STRUCTURE OF THE POEM & THE DYNAMICS OF ACTUAL SPEECH; & TRACES A "LINE" FROM THE INNOVATORS OF OUR OWN TIME & THE CENTURIES IMMEDIATELY PRECEDING, BACK BY WHATEVER ROUTES, TO REACH THE FIRST MYTHOLOGIZED SHAMANS OF THE LATER PALEOLITHIC CULTURES. I can't get it any simpler than that, & filling in the names & key events (although I've done a little of it earlier) would be to set a limit that I can't admit.

SPANOS: The "tradition" of the "school" of Eliot was given establishment status in the American universities by the New Critics in the 50s, and in the process also established an educational methodology based on the kind of tightly constructed paradoxical "metaphysical" poetry they admired. I'm referring, of course, to the ultra close reading, the *explication de texte,* of Brooks's and Warren's *Understanding Poetry,* that implies a hermeneutics that begins from the end. Do you think the frame of reference of the New Criticism is capable of reading, I mean of perceiving what's central to the oral poetry you've collected in *Technicians* and *Shaking the Pumpkin* and *America a Prophecy* or even to the emergent poetry of the new "oral" imagination—to, say, Olson's *Maximus Poems,* the poems of Creeley's *For Love* or more recently *Pieces* and *A Day Book,* or Ginsberg's *Kaddish,* or Snyder's *Earth House Hold,* or Antin's *Talking,* or your *Poland/1931?*

ROTHENBERG: My temptation here is to say "unfortunately yes." I think the "frame of reference" could be applied to the kinds of poems you mention & probably to anything else. (I won't argue its centrality as yet.) I remember that the "method" was applied, as parody, to "hickery-dickery-dock," where it was at least enjoyable. I remember too that it used to be applied to the poetry of the New Critics themselves (those who wrote poetry) & to other works far less complex than Olson's or Snyder's & less "paradoxical" than Creeley's, whose early stuff is like a kind of public Dickinson (a favorite target poet for the "method"). I don't think the "method" would apply to most of Stein, say, though if the New Critics had been as serious about "language" & "linguistics" as they claimed to be, they should have recognized her as the modern poet most serious in turn about grammar & syntax, & would have found a way to speak about her. I don't know what they might do about Antin's talking poems, except to dig the irony & take the chance of talking back—which would be more fun than what they're noted for. And I can easily imagine "New Critical" explications of my own work, but feel lucky to be living at a later time.

Not that much later, though. Where I keep thinking of the New Criticism as dead & buried with the 1950s, in regard to "primitive" & "oral" poetry, say, you do in fact have something like it in Lévi-Strauss's "structural" studies of myth. A number of the predecessors (Jakobson, & so on) are identical, & the process of reducing myth from a particular language event to a synopsis that transforms & rationalizes contradictions is very much the same. That kind of reductionism seems far from the idea of poem-as-process—rather implies that the synopsis is itself the structure: the message, so to speak, except "in other words." (I would guess that if the New Criticism were to resurface, it would be in a "structuralist" disguise.)

So here I am, already into the "unforunate" side of it—to wonder if any "study" that evades the questions of "function" & "performance" (thus turns, as you quote Olson, from "language as the act of the instant" to "language as the act of thought about the instant") can still be of much use to us. And that would be a problem, as I see it, even if the New Critics hadn't been committed to a very limited view of form &

a general conservatism about language. Poetry has rarely been composed as an occasion for criticism (the "New Critical" poets may here be an exception). It has other, very different functions for those who make it, & may (as a process) appear in situations that aren't easy to define within the framework of "literature." When it does, all kinds of factors "outside" the poem—the intention of the poet, his relation to a community, the conditions of his life & time, his politics, the claims he makes to vision or experience, & so on—all these (& more) become important, even central. And the "criticism" that doesn't recognize them, that can't, with Cage, reverse the roles of life & art (& share that life, at least by way of challenge), can only obscure the function, push the poem into a different realm, one with far less at stake.

It's no surprise either that Brooks & Warren called their book *Understanding Poetry,* since the thrust was toward "understanding" as the main activity of the reader/listener: to exploit the need to understand apart from hearing or participation. (What do you understand then?) There's a tremendous amount in fact that precedes "understanding" in that sense—particularly with oral poetry & poetry as performance. And there are poems not meant to be "understood," so to speak, as much as *presented:* offered up. The act of *sounding* the poem, like that of making it, may (as in ritual or prayer or incantation) overshadow the urge to understand it. I'm certainly not ruling "meaning" out in saying this, but it does seem to me that an unbalanced emphasis on "understanding" is a Western hang-up that has too often, in Paul Blackburn's words, "wracked all passion from the sound of speech." And you find, in returning to the "oral," in making the poem sound (& the listener hear & sound the words in turn), that if the mind is only tuned to understanding, it may miss the poem & its occasion in the effort to keep up. Poetry is too intense an event for the *New Criticism* to be more than peripheral.

And I'm saying that, remember, as a poet mad for content—let me make that clear!

SPANOS: I share your reservations about "understanding poetry"—the impulse to suspend the process of a poem for the sake of seeing (understanding) the whole poem from the end (as an object)—and your commitment to "performance," which, as I too have tried to suggest, are indeed grounded in something like Olson's distinction between "language as the act of an instant" and "language as the act of thought about the instant." What kind of "interpretive" consciousness, then, does one bring to this oral poetry that's not mediated by print? (Incidentally, a book like Robert Scholes's *Structuralism in Literature: An Introduction,* Yale University Press, 1974, goes far to verify your guess that if the New Criticism were to resurface "it would be in a structuralist disguise.") When, in *Technicians of the Sacred,* you speak of the anthology as "limit smashing," are you also proposing a radical transformation of modern reading habits? What does this mean for poetry in the college classroom, or does it mean that poetry doesn't belong in the classroom?

ROTHENBERG: First let me say that most of the new "oral" (i.e., "sounded") poetry appears in, or "is mediated by," print —but we've already spoken about that in answer to your first question.

As for poetry "belonging" in the classroom, it's like the way they taught us sex in those old hygiene classes: not performance but semiotics. If I had taken Hygiene 71 seriously, I would have become a monk; & if I had taken college English seriously, I would have become an accountant. But I do teach from time to time, so realize that the classroom becomes a substitute for those places (coffee shop or kiva) where poetry actually happens & where it can be "learned" (not "taught") in action. To shift all that into a classroom is a little like preserving a language not normally spoken by those learning it—like the Hebrew of the Americanized "talmud torahs" when I was a kid, or the efforts I've observed, by Senecas & other Indians, to maintain languages that children no longer use at home. If there isn't some carry-over, the classroom will be a burden to those entering. And the situation is the same for poetry—as long, that is, as the root activity, the function, fails to come across.

I'm not sure that "oral" poetry, & so on, offers a way out,

but if it does, the change in "instruction" would have several aspects. First off there would have to be a stress on "function": even possibly the development of some kind of anthropological approach to poetry, from the "primitive," highly functionalized uses to the literary forms in which "function" is more oblique, dependent on a changed relationship between the poet & his culture. In coming at it from the "oral" side, an effort should be made to let "life tyrannize over art," at least to bring auditors into closer contact with the situations in which poetry occurs:

: by "introducing" poetry, as far as possible, without compulsion—toward that "oral" situation, in which the novice can enter the experience, can learn by hearing & participation;

: by reference to "primitive" & other materials in which the art & life relationship is clearest (or biographical, not necessarily "psychological," information, where the social bond has broken down);

: by utilization of poets within the classroom or adjunct to it (live readings, tapes & video, & so on), to help re-establish aspects of the "tribal" situation in which poetry is learned in association with poets & other "keepers of the high words";

: by "sounding," discouraging silent readings of the text: to remember that even where poetry is "mediated by print," the mouth moves with the mind in learning;

: by having students hear & notate their own speech, compose poems & perform them, integrate them with the other "arts";

: by encouraging, to start with, a reconsideration of those forms of poetry (song & ballad, street rap, heightened speech, & so on) which may be part of the auditors' lives (i.e., the poetry they really use)—before moving on to other, less familiar kinds.

All this of course would be by way of "introduction." In the advanced study of poetry, I would again urge what I've urged so often: the expansion of the field, in line with present practice, to include the widest range of forms & poetries, & to supplement the study qua literature with other studies qua anthropology, psychology, & so on. It will be clear, if this is done, that there are responses (from ecstatic listening & participation to discussion, even challenges, of ideas & content) that are more compelling than those methods favored by the old New Critics.

SPANOS: There's no question that the attempt to emphasize the prophetic, the visionary, dimensions of the oral tradition in behalf of recovering the sacredness—"the underlying relatedness of all life," as you and Quasha put it in the introduction of *America a Prophecy*—is an important and necessary one. This is made dramatically clear when it's seen in the light of the dehumanized—to say nothing of desacralized—mentality that has made Vietnam, the Watergate, the exile of Solzhenitsyn, the representative history of modern "civilized" life. On the other hand—as it should by now be obvious—I'm uneasy about the accompanying commitment to a poetry of collage that is insistently committed to a *synchronic* sense of time, which to me implies a desire to abolish history or at any rate the consciousness of man's historicity. Let me quote in full the passage where Eliade talks about modern writers' "nostalgia for the myth of eternal repetition and, in the last analysis, for the abolition of time." And he writes, in a passage that strikes me as remarkably prophetic in the light of the emergence of this enormous interest in the oral "primitive" tradition and its uses for contemporary poetry:

At a moment when history could do what neither the cosmos, nor man, nor chance have yet succeeded in doing— that is, wipe out the human race in its entirety—it may be that we are witnessing a desperate attempt to prohibit the "events of history" through a reintegration of human societies within the horizon (artificial, because decreed) of archetypes and their repetition. In other words, it is not inadmissible to think of an epoch, and an epoch not too far distant, when humanity, to ensure its survival, will find itself reduced to desisting from any further "making" of history in the sense in which it began to make it from the creation of the first empires, will confine itself to repeating prescribed archetypal gestures, and will strive to forget, as meaningless and dangerous, any spontaneous gesture which might entail "historical" consequences. It would even be interesting to compare the anhistorical solution of future societies with the paradisal or eschatological myths of the golden age of the beginning or the end of the world.

Eliade's point of view here is, more or less, neutrally empirical (though phrases like "artifical, because decreed" give away at least his doubts as to the possibility of recovering *that time*). I quote the passage because it points specifically to what makes me uneasy about the contemporary attempt to, how shall I put it, "retribalize" poetry. How would you respond to the charge that the primitive-oriented oral poetic you're emphasizing in your work disregards the imperatives of human historicity?

ROTHENBERG: I assume that Eliade is working off the Christian distinction between "time" & "eternity" (a proposition I find meaningless) & referring to poets like Eliot who had a stake in that. In terms of my own contemporaries, I don't have a real sense of a move to "abolish" or "prohibit" history, & I certainly don't see it as inevitable to the proposals mentioned in your question. Obviously one can make "dreamtime" & "history" into an either/or situation, but that would be a result of categorical thinking & not a real response to it. A basic thrust of my own work (since I assume your challenge is directed to that) has been to re-explore the past on the basis of information that has become available to us since the nineteenth century. In doing this, I've felt my "consciousness of our historicity" increased rather than diminished. And I don't understand how a "view of history" that clings to a limited, linear image of the past along Hellenic-Hebraic, Western, even Indo-European lines can be said to be historically oriented in contrast to the "view of history" I've been offering.

The question, then, is who in fact has the desire to "prohibit" history? Who is so terrified by the rise of new forces in our world & the increased "freight of human experience" that, against all the facts & the new knowledge coming to light, they cling to a myth of European hegemony, & so on? (Here the connection between the "making of history" & "the creation of the first empires" makes me wonder if the decline of the most recent of these isn't the unstated issue behind the desire to make time stop.) And why does an emphasis on "the prophetic, the visionary . . . the underlying relatedness of all life" (in part made possible by a new historic & evolutionary consciousness) seem to be in conflict with a sense of history as something "lived" & "made"?

This is the first occasion when I've felt compelled to answer question with question, because I'm astonished that an enterprise which seems to me not only "important & necessary" but (in its emphasis on the "relatedness of all life") empirical as well, is taken as a sign of an escape from history &, by implication, from reality. I'm not saying that the methods proposed (collage & synchronicity & so on) may not be inadequate or inappropriate, but the thrust of your question seems more basic than that. And if it is, it seems to me that you're making it in spite of the fact that so much of our poetry (& the ideology behind it) represents a unique attempt (by those like Pound & Olson, but also the Surrealists, say, who learned from Marx as well as Freud) to make a poetry "including history": the re-introduction of empiricism into the center of our poems for the first time in how many centuries!

What I've spoken of so far involves history as a record of the past—by now a much expanded record—& there I don't really see a problem. But the idea of history as a process, like the idea of what time itself is, has also changed so much in this century, that the actual nostalgia seems to occur in clinging to the older linear model, feeling that if that goes, history itself goes—whatever that may mean. So, I see the process in time as non-linear & multichronic (including but not dominated by dream-time), though synchronic & simultaneous in consciousness: i.e., the mind bringing together a large number of elements from culturally & spatially separated chronologies. That's a way to deal with time, as cubism dealt with a multiplicity of spatial perspectives without, I think, denying roundedness. The idea has been to intensify our present consciousness—our sense of past & future not as distant & ourselves as alienated, but as open to our immediate & useful apprehension.

I can hardly understand what it is to be anhistorical, so I likely miss it in the work of others. But I listen carefully to an anthropologist & social historian like Stanley Diamond, who has been sympathetic to our work & tells us:

> Human consciousness is historical; in order to understand ourselves, to heal ourselves, in this age of abstract horror, we must regain the sense of the totality and the immediacy of human experience. In order to determine where we are, we must learn, syllable by syllable, where we have been. The sense of history is, for society in crisis, what relentless self-searching, psychoanalytic or otherwise, is for the individual in crisis, that is, it can be releasing and enriching, cathartic and creative; it may be the only thing that can save our lives. History implies exhortation, because it is confession, failure and triumph. It is the measure of our capacity, the link between man and man, the key to ourselves.

Or when Pound writes that *"all* ages are contemporaneous *in the mind,"* I take that as having been a useful start & underline the first word & the last three words as crucial. The danger may not be with the poets at all—may come in fact from those historians who try to reify the past, to keep it separate, since that may in itself be an evasion. I don't see that the poet's proposition (of bringing history—the past & future—into presence) evades the issue but lives it out.

SPANOS: Clearly, the literature of the absurd, which has its source in the emergence of existentialism as something like a world view since World War II, is a "post-modern" (or at least "anti-modern") phenomenon, especially in its effort to create a literary form that, unlike the formalism of the symbolist art of, say, Mallarmé or Yeats, or Eliot, engages men on one level or another *in their history.* Given your primary interest in the visionary and magical potentialities of poetry, it might seem that the post-modern imagination or, at any rate, the post-modern literary scene, is characterized by a radical split between its impulse to enter history and to transcend history. Yet each has in common a total revolt against the causal and rigidly linear temporality (beginning, middle, and end) of the coercive positivistic imagination and the "totalitarian" technological city it has produced. Is the "post-modern" imagination in fact divided against itself? Or can you see some connection between such contemporary existentialists and absurdists as Sartre, Beckett, Ionesco, Genet, Pinter, Barth, and Pynchon—who also, by the way, are obsessed by the question of language and, in some cases, are trying to recover the *Logos* as speech—and the post-modernism you're articulating in your poetry, theoretic statements, and your visionary editing?

ROTHENBERG: I think I've covered most of this already, but there are still some points I want to respond to or make clearer. The "world view" in question, if it's that, is more post-"symbolist" than it is post-"modernist," &, along with the "question of language" & "the LOGOS as speech," is a principle link between what you present here as disconnected movements. My own discomfort isn't with the "symbols" *per se* (though I read them as "images" & that makes quite a difference) but with that "symbolism" which substitutes interpretation for presentation: the kind of distinction that put the surrealists into conflict with the symbolists & the New Critics with the surrealists, & so on. The surrealist "image" is unmediated, its associations implicit & directly perceived, as in the experience of "dream," which was of course their model. In that sense I've always assumed a continuity between the Surrealists & the absurdists—with someone like Kafka or Breton, say, in his collections of "black humor," as an intermediary figure. For the absurdists the idea of the absurd itself (like "dream" for the surrealists) serves as the great simplifying concept, which allows for a direct presentation of conflicting impulses. This immediacy (which is also the issue in post-symbolist collage, in automatic writing, systematic chance, projective verse, objectivism, concrete & sound poetry, & so on) seems more central to me than the formalism/non-formalism you presume to see as marking the symbolist/anti-symbolist split. (I also see it as more critical than the "subjective"/"objective" splits within the post-symbolist scene, since those have generally been mediated by concepts like Olson's "proprioception" or Zukofsky's favoring of "the clear physical eye against the erring brain.") But I differ from you, remember, in that I think the move away from symbolism is characteristic of modern poetry from World War I to World War II, though not clearly articulated or divested of symbolist traces until the 1950s. . . .

So, the fundamental division, as I understand it, is along the axis described. I would emphasize that division by all means, while playing down (for the moment at least) the post-symbolist differences: not "a house divided against itself" but contemporaries working toward mutual completion. The model in my own case has been, increasingly, the so-called "primitive" or "ethnopoetic"—at least as the "myth of the primitive" has been developed over the last two centuries—& that myth, at least as I've gone at it, has been of an essentially non-symbolist situation, in which chance, concretism, vision, even the absurd, aren't separate impulses but part of a larger "world view." If you read *Technicians* carefully (& don't confuse me throughout with Eliade), you'll see that I really don't tend to symbolize in that, but as far as I can, by selection & arrangement, to present the poetry in immediately apprehensible terms. (Obviously, where I'm also quoting a range of earlier commentators, I can't be really consistent—but then I've never taken consistency as a fundamental value.) And, to get back to what started off your question, I think I clearly imply, though I may not directly state, a connection or parallel between the "absurd," say, & something like Malinowski's "coefficient of weirdness" [see below, page 144] as part of the myth of primal consciousness & language. It is, let me say, central to my own thought & work—right up through *Poland* & *A Seneca Journal*—& I prize the old shamans & the oral poets as much for that as for the transcendental symbols, & so on, which to me are meaningless without it.

SPANOS: . . . It's pretty clear from your acknowledgment of contradiction, of the particulars of immediate experience, your continuing commitment to "making it new"—from your last remarks in general—that the kinds of poetry you include in your definition of an alternative "tradition" neither have their source in an effort to transcend the real world, "to arrest and raise the mind above desire and loathing" as Stephen Dedalus calls the kinetic realm of historicity, nor do they take any obvious form of object-ivization. On the other hand, one could conclude, if he did not pay careful attention, from much that you have said about poetry and the tradition (i.e., the centrality of myth, which may be defined as a "world picture" or "world mosaic," that *places* and thus neutralizes contingency) and from the way you say it (i.e., the powerful—and astonishing—assimilative or analogical quality of your argument or, perhaps better, the inclusive impulse of your imagination) that, in spite of your commitment to a poetic *tradition* of "changes," you tend to conceive the particular poem (and the history of poetic utterance) in spatial terms, so that the word "oral" does not preclude closed or pre-determined forms. Can I go back once more to that identification of "eye" with "I" to ask you to amplify, in the context of this phenomenological critique of symbolist/imagist modernism (if not of modernism at large), on your understanding of the relationship between oral poetry and your visual (or visionary) emphasis? In other words, how would you distinguish between the iconic or spatial poem of the symbolist/imagist tradition (as I've defined it) and the "oral" poem envisioned in your definition of the alternative tradition?

ROTHENBERG: This reminds me of one of those hypothetical questions as to which of our senses we would rather do without. I always assume I'm not being prodded toward an actual deprivation, but in the present instance I'm not all that sure. I don't know, anyway, if I can make more than scattered comments in response.

(1) In a truly oral culture (which is not what ours is), there are no mute poets & probably no deaf poets.* In some

* From a later vantage, I would have to feed into this statement some sense of the culture or sub-culture of the deaf, which has begun to produce a contemporary signing poetry that calls into question the purely oral (speaking-hearing) basis of much of our poetics. But all of that awaits a future reading. (J.R., 6/1/80)

44

cultures there have been *blind* poets, including some deliberately blinded. But it isn't clear whether this was to intensify the other senses (or speech & memory) or to turn sight inward. (Maybe it was to keep the poets from running off.)

(2) For myself, I think, in spite of the blind Homers, that eye-orientation isn't Western but human—back even to the earliest primates, when the muzzle shrank & the eyes moved forward in the skull. The consequent adjustment of the brain toward vision made of puny man a hunter & a seer. It "defined" thought & imagination (imaging) just as speech "defined" poetry. But not so neatly either: the two, I mean, aren't separated in real life, & in any sane society would be thought of as inseparable. (If you'll look at that neat phrase in your last sentence—"the 'oral' poem envisioned"—you'll see that your own language allows the possibility of saying what I mean.)

(3) Blake, as a "prophet" of the new poetry, called for an opening of *all* the senses; at the same time he demanded a freeing of speech & verse ("Poetry Fetter'd, Fetters the Human Race!") & developed it further in practice. I see this as a totalization of energy: anything less already represents a form of entropy.

(4) But assuming, as you seem to, that "visual" & "oral" involve a contradiction, it may be just that contradiction which is the basis of the tension that informs our poetry. This tension, as you describe it further, is between "repose" & "flux"— both of which, to borrow again from Blake, "are necessary to human existence." As a poet I can sustain such contradictions; in prose I'm helpless to conclude the conversation.

(5) To force a choice, one way or the other, where contradiction is irreducible, would be the intention of thought devoid of dialectic. This, it seems to me, is the real issue, in poetry as elsewhere. I would, anyway, be very careful about disposing of "modernists" or "post-modernists" because they seem at any point to be favoring the "wrong" side of the dialectic. (Do dialectics have wrong sides?) If you do that, you end up with very little, earlier in the century or now.

(6) But to get to specific cases: I'm concerned, e.g., about the too easy linkage of "symbolism" and "imagism," as if to

ignore the latter's attack on the former or that one of its key proposals (at least in Pound's or Williams's formulation) was to restore speech as the poetic ground. (What poet was into that restoration who wasn't also identifying as a "modernist"?) There are some complex figures operative here, i.e., who were exploring, working, several ways at once. And while I hate to keep saying it, the clincher for me is still how often the "visual" & "oral" openings appear in the work of the same individual—from Blake or Whitman to the very present. The articulation of that is unprecedented, except back to the oral/visionary cultures.

So I have no doubt, e.g., that Pound, as he emerges from the 19th century, carries some of the symbolist baggage with him. But the idea of *image* (as "direct treatment of the 'thing' " or "an intellectual/emotional complex in an instant of time" or "vortex") is, along with the other dicta of his "imagism (e)," already away from "symbolism" & toward "a language conceived as speech, the act of an instant." (I assume that one who speaks that language isn't sightless.) Or, to cite a further inconsistency: if Stein is an early modernist concerned with the "act of the instant" (& she is with her "continuous present," & so on), she is also the one most into a "cubist" poetics. What's attractive in fact is just that double concern—for "flux" & "timeless picture"—whether in her *Four Saints,* say, or in the works of other cubist artists. And Stein, our one great "cubist" poet, is the direct American predecessor to many of the poets you identify as *post*-modernists (Antin, Cage, Mac Low, & so on), just as Pound is to most of the others.

If we're going to be empirical & into history, we might as well indulge a little rage for chaos—at least that nothing in the real world is that tidy. And right there is my argument with post-modernism as a discrete category: that without a sense of continuities (from such as Pound & Stein & so on) the "break" from modernism may itself be exploited against the post-modernists you name. So it's not that we aren't done with symbolism—unless we find some other use for it—but that the effort to divide speech & sight on our behalf is a further instance of that literal or linear thinking that has always sold us short. The paradigm, in other words, remains totalization, which means in our time that no single-aspect art can have more than a few years' currency, unless it's seen within the larger framework.

(7) A poetry of changes is a poetry of contradictions, i.e., of the dialectical imagination, perspective by incongruity, & so on. The world in which we live lies between formlessness & form: it shapes itself at each pass we make, & we who are changing as well are called on again & again to remake it. The variety of our ways (& the recognition of the will to change) defines our modernism—our living in this time. And hopefully as we go on, we can accelerate the process rather than repeat what will become more & more rigid pictures of the real. Certainly the grubbiness of contingency has been more appealing to later than to early modernism—has, in my view of it, kept us more honestly human. However that may be, we're now able to draw from predecessors confronted by the same necessities. These include earlier modernists & "primitives," along with a range of other human beings, poets of all times & places, who remind us that we're neither the first poets nor will we be the last.

Boundary 2, Volume III, Number 3, Spring 1975.

2 / Pre-Faces & Manifestos

I will change your mind.

A PERSONAL MANIFESTO (1966)

1) I will change your mind;
2) any means (= methods) to that end;
3) to oppose the "devourers" = bureaucrats, system-makers, priests, etc. (W. Blake);
4) "& if thou wdst understand that wch is me, know this: all that I have sd I have uttered playfully—& I was by no means ashamed of it." (J. C. to disciples, *The Acts of St. John*)

From DEEP IMAGE & MODE:
AN EXCHANGE WITH ROBERT CREELEY (1960)

[*By the late 1950s my own first discoveries (along with immediate contemporaries such as Kelly, Schwerner, Economou, Eshleman, Wakoski) surfaced in a series of propositions & compositional experiments dealing with what I was then calling "deep image" & would describe later as "a power, among several, by which the poem is sighted & brought close." The heated & still open atmosphere of those years evoked a number of re-enforcements &/or questionings (Snyder, Duncan, Creeley, Antin, Levertov, Bly, et al.) that helped to keep the work surprising & to remind us all of the actual complexity of the processes at hand. The background—sometimes slighted in the effort to assert a "difference"—was from the earlier avant-gardes & from those anonymous tribal & subterranean predecessors whose voices were to figure so largely in my later work. Of the exchange with Creeley I wrote: "The letters that follow are conclusive without reaching any conclusions. They begin & end with two divergent positions which are, in the process, juxtaposed, placed one upon the other, so that from the overlay—as in some well-known color process in photography—a third, perhaps richer view emerges. . . . If we start from two different positions, are we lining up for battle, taking sides? . . . Or will the 'truth' finally be found in some poem, in the poems that are made or put into motion by, among other things, just such encounters as these? Is the truth not at every place where we treasure the reality of our actions in the world with a painful awareness?" Reprinted here are Creeley's first response to my book* White Sun Black Sun *& to Robert Kelly's "Notes on the Poetry of Image," & the first two letters in which I try to set a ground for my still developing concerns & to respond to the invitations implicit in his own positions.*]

Dear Jerry,

Thank you very much for the copy of your book—which seems to me very handsome and clear. Thanks too for the copy of Robert Kelly's notes. As yourself I find them interesting. I think, however, that this concept of "image" becomes very general, i.e., generalizes, pretty quickly. E.g., "The clothed percept is the image." This is too vague for me, since I feel that speaking, or writing, itself becomes a "percept" and in this guise a deep influence on the "thing said."

More particularly, as a contrast, read Williams' notes on Zukofsky at the back of *A*, i.e., Williams speaks of his own sometimes bewilderment at Z/s intent, i.e., "The poems whatever else they are are grammatical units intent on making a meaning *unrelated* to a mere pictorial image." I know that Kelly has more in mind than that, i.e., "pictorial image," and yet I feel he consciously or not uses the "picture" as base term from which his sense of "image" derives. That is, I feel he means all to be shaped to the term of an "image" (picture), the "verbalized image" as he says. In my own sense, there is an "image" in a mode, in a *way* of statement as much "image" as any reference to pictorial element, e.g. the white night, the color of sorrow, etc. Pictorial image there relates of course as any other element, but to my mind not as importantly as rhythm, or the structure in which rhythm may operate freely— as a "poem" etc. Again as a parallel to these concerns, Zukofsky writes apropos some poems sent him: "[one is best] when the analysis comes thru the lyrical; the danger of *The Woman* and *The Plan* is that the analysis sometimes becomes melodramatic; on the other hand, getting an image by something like the privation of it or transformation of it thru the physiology of the sound and cadence counteracts it—the melodrama . . ." It is that Kelly describes all this question of mode too briefly, i.e., "The image is the measure of the line. The line is cut to fit it . . ." Of course, but in quite what sense? Isn't then the image as much that cut, of line, as it is what that cut of line makes, of a reference, pictorial or otherwise? That's where I tend to wander. I cannot agree to that which does not place great emphasis upon structure—in all possible reaches, certainly in Kelly's also—and so again feel the problem which something even as careful as this seems to lead to.

For example, take the discussion of that line from your own poem, in which he drops the "No!" i.e., the first word in the line, in this case syllable, itself an exclamation, and so obviously of some inevitable weight in the whole term of said line.* I at least wondered, i.e., what is a "line" if you can drop such a word, and then calculate its measure. I don't follow that.

But I don't want to spend the whole letter with such apparent quibbling, i.e., you'll see simply enough wherein I am bothered—and why I can't quite agree.

The whole presence of this sense of image bothers me a little, in present work. I hope I understand what lacks, as Robert Bly might speak of them, are pointed out—but I don't honestly feel them as a lack, and/or believe poetry to encompass a great many manners and emphases, from "epic" to "lyric," and feel of course that in each a dominance will be aimed at for this or that aspect of the so-called whole. I think translation, dealt with too loosely, has not been able to surmount the problem of logopoeia, and this has made an accumulation of loosely structured poems exciting mainly for their "content," their reference as "pictures" of states of feeling etc. I'd hate to see that generalizing manner become dominant, no matter the great relief of having such information about what's being written in other countries etc. But I wouldn't back an inch off the need for as craftsmanlike poems as possible, not at all meaning "tidy" etc. We are too far along, in many grounds so-called, now, to back off, e.g., from Ginsberg in opening KADDISH sections, to Dorn's long line in THE AIR OF JUNE, to O'Hara's casual line, or Duncan's

* From the poem, "Invincible Flowers" in *White Sun Black Sun*. The full line reads: "No! Give me plastic flowers, flowers in granite and ice . . ." while Kelly in his essay reprints it with the "No!" omitted.

formal organization of "canto" structure in **POEM BEGIN-NING WITH A LINE BY PINDAR**—Olson's **MAXIMUS** and "field," Williams' late poems, etc. i.e., it seems a bad time to lose sight of those areas. It would make a poet like Corso if he might learn them. It makes Burroughs, in prose, singular in his ability. So . . .

I am grateful to see the book, and very happy that you have it out—i.e., it's an interesting beginning in no sense "polite" (for me to say so), and you will take it from there god knows. Anyhow figure my worry as follows: that the "imagists" had in mind a sharp registration of an "objective" substance, be it tree or woman's mouth, an avoidance of general words etc.—and that proved dull once accomplished, i.e., the poems got awfully quick and then glib and finally banal in their laconic method—they left a lot out because they could only concentrate upon the "quick picture" etc. Now "image" becomes an involvement with the psychology of reference, what the preoccupation with structure tended to forget (and so became often dry in its lack of "content," simply a machine of manner etc.)—but I wonder if image can be isolated in this way, or if it will not tend to make sensational reference overvalued. This is the aspect of surrealism to me least interesting for example—the scarey parts (however interesting on first contact etc.). Anyhow that's what's on my mind.

All my best to you.
Bob

New York

November 14, 1960

Dear Bob,

I appreciate greatly the concern in your last letter about the implications of our speaking of new ways into the poem through image, etc. Since I approach my own assumptions with unrest and deep-down doubts, for you to raise questions from out there will hardly appear as "quibbling" or "picking away." God knows, if we're to bother with anything like the "truth" of what we say—and make it (somehow) a place of meeting—we shouldn't resist the clear, hard statement of our differences, but determine where we now stand to later find each other. In picking up the thread, then, I want to avoid for now trying simply to fit my position to what I read as your attitudes, vocabulary, etc. (doesn't accommodation or equivocation for the sake of agreement only distort and alter what the real point is?) and to attempt rather to let the differences emerge.

You're right that "pictorial image" is not what's in mind (the imagists largely beside the point in this), but something else that may start there only to emerge as different in the poem—i.e. the movement (action) of the poem. I've used the term "deep image" to mark out the difference, and Kelly's revised Notes follow through on this. Definition makes me a little dizzy—feeling the danger, I mean, of being trapped in a (theoretical) limitation too easily arrived at. So, for myself, the method (as in *Floating World*)* has been to explain by example (in selection of the poems) and suggestion (in the appended prose-statements). If I try now, it's not as anything final, rather to make the leap and falter, hoping something of value will be reached in the end.

To speak quickly, I connect "deep image" with *perception as an instrument of vision*, i.e. a visionary consciousness opening through the senses, grasping the phenomenal world not only for its outward form (though this also, of necessity) but winning from a compassionate comprehension of that world a more acute, more agonizing view of reality than by rational interpretation, etc. ("Psychology of reference" seems to me to limit the possibilities implied here, which should be left free to develop beyond the closed subjective, etc.)

> Nor is the idea brand new: Blake (and Smart before him) having practiced something like it before the 19th century—the deep image sud-

* *Poems from the Floating World:* magazine published by J. R. from 1959 to 1963.

denly there and (even stranger) emerging in open or free forms (not only long-line "biblical" either)— plus an awareness of what the problem was: "If the doors of perception were cleansed every thing would appear to man as it is, infinite. For man has closed himself up, till he sees all things thru narrow chinks of his cavern."

Even more closely put in "There Is No Natural Religion" and "All Religions are One."

And elsewhere:
"How do you know but every Bird
        that cuts the airy way
Is an immense world of delight,
        closed by your senses five?"

So there are really two things here, conceivable as two realities: 1) the empirical world of the naïve realists, etc. (what Buber and the hasidim call "shell" or "husk"), and 2) the hidden (floating) world, yet to be discovered or brought into being: the "kernel" or "sparks." The first world both hides and leads into the second, so as Buber says: "one cannot reach the kernel of the fruit except thru the shell"; i.e. the phenomenal world is to be read by us: the perceived image is the key to the buried image: and the deep image is at once husk and kernel, perception and vision, and the poem is the movement between them.

(I don't mean to say, by the way, that there are no other ways of conceiving "the poem": enough to think here of what might be called "deep image poem" or "visionary poem.")

Form, then, must be considered here as emerging from the act of vision: completely organic. Olson too in Projective Verse (tho differently oriented) seems to say the same: why I find it surprising when other projectivists treat it almost as a closed system. But I don't want to get into that, at least not till I've put it in my own terms.

57

Form, to my mind, is the pattern of the movement from perception to vision: it arises as the poem arises and has no life outside the movement of the poem, i.e. outside the poem itself. (This implies too that the experience of the poet, unlike that of the mystic, is patterned and developmental, i.e. expressive; the mystic, so I'm told, may not even be said to be seeking a vision of reality, but absorption within it—silence rather than speech. But mystics are close to visionary consciousness and are often poets themselves.)

So, two things at least describe for me the "new" imagination beginning with Blake, Whitman, etc.: 1) the idea of perception as an instrument of vision, and 2) of form as organic (a pattern of total movement, inseparable from that movement). So, if you isolate Kelly's statement "the line is cut to fit the images," I would agree that it doesn't hold. No more than to say "the image is cut to fit the line." (But just before that he's said: "the image and the line structure cannot be chosen and built up independently," which makes me tend to read the words you quote differently.)

But I don't want either to simplify the problem of composition by reducing it to automatism, something beyond the poet's will. (What's called "automatic writing" reads to me like confused consciousness rather than any kind of penetration.) While the breakthrough, the real poem, seems often simply to occur ("in a flash of light," Yeats says), the condition of its occurrence, before and after, is that of real freedom, so the poet can control and create. (Imagination, too, must be free to overcome the merely rational order of perception and drive it toward vision.) Even beyond the first emergence, it seems to me possible to break the immediate structure for the sake of heightened vision, to force a deeper opening, etc. Anyway one isn't simply a prisoner of what comes first, since freedom in the poem is total and the exercise of freedom extends beyond the first sighting, etc. But a basic structure—where the poem has come well—seems to me to inhere from the beginning, and to change the patterns of line or sound arbitrarily (i.e. in disregard of vision) is to damage the totality. (Conversely any later re-casting of image would force a change in line, etc.)

To bring it together thus far, the following (roughly) would be the "principles" on which I stand:

> The poem is the record of a movement from perception to vision.
> Poetic form is the pattern of that movement through space and time.
> The deep image is the content of vision emerging in the poem.
> The vehicle of movement is imagination.
> The condition of movement is freedom.

Having reached here, I'm aware of many specific things still to be said, but feel that to push it much further would be to dam up the possibilities of new development, or open the way really for the imagist banality you spoke of. Huidobro (naming himself a "creationist") saw the genius of the new poetry in its power to create rather than imitate (each poem a new creation, not a copy of nature or of other poems), which seems to me to place a maximum value on the unique differences between poets, as all have different eyes and minds; i.e. the important thing is not to make a school, but to hope for a refocusing of concern toward a "deeper" view, a departure from the merely literal, from the imitation or simple description of experience, a breaking down of perceptual limitations, a sense of urgency and desperation in the assault on reality— all matters of spirit and energy, of inner direction. (I mean here that even beyond "deep image," etc., is the overriding force of Blake's "poetic genius" (daemon) or Lorca's "duende" —simply, perhaps, passion acting on things.)

Other things too I'd like to speak of, many suggested directly by your letter or earlier correspondence with Duncan, Snyder, etc., talks with Kelly, Schwerner, and others here: the role of imagination (the power to freely associate perceptions—probably the main link, or only link, with the surrealists that Bly makes so much of); the question of limiting vocabulary, etc. (I think in terms of an empirical language, not simply the concrete words of the imagists); the difference between deep image and Yeats's symbols, Jungian archetypes, etc.; the important question you raise about "mode" as image; the naming of origins (not only beginning with Blake, but back into ancient texts); etc. etc.

Well, having got started I now take a deep breath and put all else off for a 2nd letter, hoping I haven't taken liberties in writing so much now; only that the questions were real and the desire to get something off held back for too long a time. Write as you can, tho I can't hide that I look forward to more from you. I'll pick this up on my own in a few days, if all goes well.

Best as ever,
Jerry

New York

November 28, 1960

Dear Bob—

I hesitated for some time before sending off the last letter, wondering if, without addressing myself to the question of the poem as an aural entity, etc., the rest would not still seem vague and generalized. Finally decided to let it go and continue with this.

To begin with, I pretty much agree that in some sense "speaking, or writing, itself becomes a 'percept' and in this guise a deep influence on the 'thing said.'" I'd only want to qualify it by speaking of two kinds of percept: a) what you call "mode," etc. which is, to my mind, *percept internal to the poem,* and b) the *referential percepts* (image etc.) which at least seem to have external counterparts i.e., can be taken in that sense as direct analogues to meaning, reality, etc. (The latter might also include the sense of an actual dialogue in time— percept internal to the speaker—that's so strong in your own work; or should that be considered as different again? Well . . .) It seems to me that such distinctions, which I feel necessary for clarity, could again make one infer that image is prior to line or rhythm (or vice versa), yet this is deceptive—from the first opening into the poem, the referential elements are themselves sounds or patterns of sound and pulse, etc., so that it's still possible to think of the emergence of the whole poem (sound and "content") as a concurrent unity. Something like this, anyway, is how I'd want to consider "form" in the poem: as a progression and patterning of all the elements of language and vision integral to the poem's organic movement.

Well, to get to the problem of "craft" from another direction—Duncan in a letter somewhere—to Kelly or me, I forget which—asked how we'd distinguish the poem from any other visions? I think we would, of course, almost too simply, "because the poem is the vision of a poet," i.e. by here reintroducing the concept of the Makar.* But if poems are to be the visions of Makaris, they must be of Makaris who see. In other words, I don't think we should be trapped into a hasty equation of poetry and verse-making, and that's what I see as the danger where structure and/or measure are treated as isolated factors, i.e. abstractly. (Or if you're going to make this your focus, reducing the poem to sound and/or manner, shouldn't you take it as far as Stein did? The referential area of a poem, when present but neglected, has a way of turning back on the poet, betraying him into an apparent triviality.)

So, my concern so far is whether the internal percepts, when separated from vision (particularly where referential elements persist) can really lead to a poetry in depth. For myself, I feel image (free referential percept) central in this sense, as focus, if only that I still believe in this, from moment to moment can take the naïve world on faith, to move from there. (And if I lost the referential percepts also, would turn perhaps to something almost music, dropping the content altogether.) But to take form as center (in a poem that retains referential elements) seems to me almost necessarily to act toward a distortion or weakening of vision: since vision (to invert and paraphrase Zukofsky) often involves the assertion of form thru something like privation of it, or by its consideration as in-

* Scots word for poet (plural: Makaris), as it turns up in William Dunbar's "Lament for the Makers," etc.

separable from the referential percepts which it voices. But maybe it's all a question of what one stresses to begin with.

It's come to me here, having taken it this far along the first two lines mentioned, that it's really the 3rd thing—sense of a dialogue in time—that most strongly concerns you. Somehow, probably because of the emphasis Duncan put on it in earlier letters, I'd read your speaking-and-writing-as-itself-percept in terms of so-called Melos, which I suppose is implied there but not really key. Do I read you right to say you conceive of "mode" as the reality of the poem at a given point in time: the structure, perhaps, of its emergence into speech? If so, would the poem's tension be seen resulting from the almost physical effort to voice it, to make it actual? hence organic to the conceptual impulse, etc.? This, anyway, is something I can confirm from my own experience of it, though I don't believe that there's no other way in, or that the movement toward image isn't derived from the same source. What confuses me is the apparent equation of this with craft; at least I find it possible to consider craft in various ways, depending on the poem: the poem's being fashioned to do what it's about, which may be other than the presentation of a thinking-out-loud. I mean, I can't deny the validity of poems that are largely a kind of thinking-out-loud (and most good poems are that somewhere in their history), but feel this again as too narrow a center, leading to "dry manner" or substanceless psychological oozings, the sense of a great strain directed toward the statement of nothing. (And in your own work, I find this often averted precisely as the content emerges, moving toward an intense fullness: and in THE DOOR, etc. being transformed into a total poetry, which I would praise sans slightest hesitation.)

You raise a question about translation, its supposed dangers, etc., which I take it is with reference to use of it in *Fifties*,* *Floating World,* elsewhere. I obviously can't go along with you here, since I wouldn't ever have given that much time to translation as simply "informational." I think we can agree

* Robert Bly's magazine, *The Fifties,* then about to change its name to *The Sixties,* etc.

about key areas of the poem not really being "translatable" (the logopoeia, the thinking-out-loud element, etc.) if you're speaking of giving equivalents in any way exact. But precisely this is what makes it ever really worth bothering: an area left open in which (sometimes) a new poem can be written. This involves some sense of re-creation: sympathetic submergence into the generalized circumstances of the original, etc. But aside from this I think there's an area of poem that's much more nearly (tho not completely) translatable, of image, etc.: so I'd be disagreeing with the old Frost chestnut of poetry being what's lost, or only that. Anyway, I feel it's for us to cut across boundaries where we can: I'm too much out of it ever to be a nationalist, even in poetry, and while I draw a lot from where I stand (especially the structure of language, as order of the speech I know), believe we have to learn to talk also across the level of "deep image" and vision: and where the practice of it's grown rusty in present surroundings, will look to see it done wherever it's open to me and then—transforming as far as I can the part that would be lost—to hear it back in my own voice, etc.

I've been warned too, but would strongly disagree, that certain of these elements are so locked in, say, the Spanish tradition and "climate" as to be unusable by poets here. Yet Neruda's Chile isn't Lorca's Spain, more I gather like Norway in terrain and with mixtures of Basques, Indians, Celts, etc.; so too for Celan's Germany and/or Rumania, Breton's Paris, Lawrence's England, the America that's given us the sometimes emergence of this in Whitman (out of the fuzzier depths of Emerson), Stevens ("hunting tigers in red weather"), even Pound ("Thou art a beaten dog beneath the hail, A swollen magpie in a fitful sun / Half black half white"): most of our good poets somewhere in their work, yourself included. So it's these elements that move across languages, in contrast to those that inhere, that we must also keep ourselves open to see. Our tradition even now is great enough to hold whatever new approaches we bring to it, if only we fit them in with passion, etc. In the next *Floating World,* too, I've tried to include a few "ancient" texts translated into the native idiom but with the image kept strong or even re-enforced: all of this with the feeling that there's other ways into the poem than what we've so far gotten from Pound and Williams: other ways too of music and craft: and ultimately that each of us must come to his own "truth," etc. from whatever direction: the unique coherence and rightness of each poem. . . .

As ever,

Jerry

Kulchur, Volume 2, Number 6, Summer 1962.

REVOLUTIONARY PROPOSITIONS (1966)

1.

A revolution involves a change in structure; a change in style is not a revolution.

2.

A revolution in poetry or painting or music is part of a total revolutionary pattern. (Modern) art is fundamentally subversive. Its thrust is toward an open-ended (continuous) revolution.

3.

"Any form whatever, by the mere fact that it exists as such & endures, necessarily loses vigor & becomes worn; to recover vigor, it must be reabsorbed into the formless if only for an instant; it must be restored to the primordial unity from which it issued; in other words, it must return to 'chaos' (on the cosmic plane), to 'orgy' (on the social plane), to 'darkness' (for seed), to 'water' (baptism on the human plane, Atlantis on the plane of history, and so on)."—*M. Eliade*

4.

"The tree of liberty must be refreshed from time to time with the blood of patriots & tyrants. It is its natural manure."—*T. Jefferson.* "Without contraries is no progression. Attraction & Repulsion, Reason & Energy, Love & Hate, are necessary to Human Existence."—*W. Blake*

5.

It is possible to rationalize the history of modern poetry or art, to mask its subversive character; but even as fad & fashion, poetry continues to subvert, to destroy the constructs of an old order as it builds the shadow-constructs of a new one.

6.

"The development of the five senses is the work of the entire history of the world up to now."—*K. Marx*

7.

A change in vision is a change in form. A change in form is a change of reality.

8.

"The poet's function is to spread doubt & create illusion."—*N. Calas*

(Second Series)

1.

Revolutions are preceded & accompanied by a breakdown in communication.

2.

Long-lived societies, even where rooted in social injustice, will survive as long as groups that should be in conflict share a common language—i.e. a common system of values & ascribed meaning, a common religion, mythology, etc.

3.

Where change (mobility) becomes so rapid as to make it impossible for the "language" to change commensurately, this common language begins to break down, & groups of men, while using the same words, no longer understand each other.

4.

This breakdown in communication is first articulated by a poet & carried on by other poets.

5.

Non-poets freely adapt the language of poets, even where they fail to understand it, to provide them with a revolutionary form of communication. They soon come to consider it their own invention.

Note. This is the history of Christianity & of the French & Russian revolutions.

6.

The poet sees the breakdown in communication as a condition of health, as an opening-up of the closed world of the old order. He carries the revolution of language & form into the new society of the political revolutionaries.

7.

The political revolutionary sees the breakdown in communication as further evidence of the malaise of the old order & dedicates himself to the re-establishment of a closed system he (or those he speaks for) can control. The demand for closure extends to the work of the poet.

8.

The confrontation between poet & political revolutionary moves toward a showdown that the poet seems fated to lose. But their lasting union would signal a turning of history & the reconstitution of Man in Eden.

Note. The sign of the Communal Paradise will be that all the languages now spoken by Man will have been made obsolete. This is the prophecy of Apollinaire.

[The preceding collage of propositions was read at a symposium on "Revolutions & Revolutionaries in Literature" at the Long

67

*Island University International Writers Conference in 1966.
Although the process described has now gone much further,
I'm even less sure about the alternative conclusion I let dangle
in the eighth proposition of the second series. Enough to say
that governments by nature (including post-revolutionary gov-
ernments once they're governing) have had little actual use for
the concept of an ongoing & open-ended revolution. But that's
all the more reason for the poets to get on with it.]*

I'kon, Number 7, January–February 1969.

PRE-FACE I:
TECHNICIANS OF THE SACRED (1968)

Primitive Means Complex

That there are no primitive languages is an axiom of con-
temporary linguistics where it turns its attention to the remote
languages of the world. There are no half-formed languages,
no underdeveloped or inferior languages. Everywhere a de-
velopment has taken place into structures of great complexity.
People who have failed to achieve the wheel will not have
failed to invent & develop a highly wrought grammar. Hunters
& gatherers innocent of all agriculture will have vocabularies
that distinguish the things of their world down to the finest
details. The language of snow among the Eskimos is awesome.
The aspect system of Hopi verbs can, by a flick of the tongue,
make the most subtle kinds of distinction between different
types of motion.

What is true of language in general is equally true of poetry
& of the ritual-systems of which so much poetry is a part. It is
a question of energy & intelligence as universal constants &, in
any specific case, the direction that energy & intelligence
(= imagination) have been given. No people today is newly
born. No people has sat in sloth for the thousands of years of
its history. Measure everything by the Titan rocket & the tran-
sistor radio, & the world is full of primitive peoples. But once
change the unit of value to the poem or the dance-event or the
dream (all clearly artifactual situations) & it becomes apparent
what all those people have been doing all those years with all
that time on their hands.

Poetry, wherever you find it among the "primitives"* (lit-

* The word "primitive" is used with misgivings & put in quotes, but
no way around it seems workable. "Non-technological" & "non-literate,"
which have often been suggested as alternatives, are too emphatic in
pointing to supposed "lacks" &, though they feel precise to start with, are
themselves open to question. Are the Eskimo snow-workers, e.g., really

erally *everywhere*), involves an extremely complicated sense of materials & structures. Everywhere it involves the manipulation (fine or gross) of multiple elements. If this isn't always apparent, it's because the carry-over (by translation or interpretation) necessarily distorts where it chooses some part of the whole that it can meaningfully deal with. The work is foreign & its complexity is often elusive, a question of gestalt or configuration, of the angle from which the work is seen. If you expect a primitive work to be simple or naïve, you will probably end up seeing a simple or naïve work; & this will be abetted by the fact that translation can, in general, only present as a single work a part of what is actually there. The problem is fundamental for as long as we approach these works from the outside—& we're likely fated to be doing that forever.

It's very hard in fact to decide what precisely are the boundaries of "primitive" poetry or of a "primitive" poem, since there's often no activity differentiated as such, but the words or vocables are part of a larger total "work" that may go on for hours, even days, at a stretch. What we would separate as music & dance & myth & painting is also part of that work, & the need for separation is a question of "our" interest & preconceptions, not of "theirs." Thus the picture is immediately complicated by the nature of the work & the media that comprise it. And it becomes clear that the "collective" nature of primitive poetry (upon which so much stress has been placed despite the existence of individualized poems & clearly identified poets) is to a great degree inseparable from the amount of materials a single work may handle.

"non"- or "pre-technological"? And how does the widespread use of pictographs & pictosymbols, which can be "read" by later generations, affect their users' non-literate status? A major point throughout this book is that these peoples (& they're likely too diverse to be covered by a single name) are precisely "technicians" where it most concerns them—specifically in their relation to the "sacred" as something they can actively create or capture. That's the only way in fact that I'd hope to define "primitive": as a situation in which such conditions flourish & in which the "poets" are (in Eliade's phrase) the principal "technicians of the sacred."

Now all of this is, if so stated, a question of technology as well as inspiration; & we may as well take it as axiomatic for what follows that where poetry is concerned, "primitive" means complex.

What Is a "Primitive" Poem?

Poems are carried by the voice & are sung or chanted in specific situations. Under such circumstances, runs the easy answer, the "poem" would simply be the words-of-the-song. But a little later on the question arises: what *are* the words & where do they begin & end? The translation, as printed, may show the "meaningful" element only, often no more than a single, isolated "line"; thus

A splinter of stone which is white (Bushman)
Semen white like the mist (Australian)
My-shining-horns (Chippewa: single word)
etc.

but in practice the one "line" will likely be repeated until its burden has been exhausted. (Is it "single" then?) It may be altered phonetically & the words distorted from their "normal" forms. Vocables with no fixed meanings may be intercalated. All of these devices will be creating a greater & greater gap between the "meaningful" residue in the translation & what-was-actually-there. We will have a different "poem" depending where we catch the movement, & we may start to ask: Is something within this work the "poem," or is everything?

Again, the work will probably not end with the "single" line & its various configurations—will more likely be preceded & followed by other lines. Are all of these "lines" (each of considerable duration) separate poems, or are they the component parts of a single, larger poem moving toward some specific (ceremonial) end? Is it enough, then, if the lines happen in succession & aren't otherwise tied? Will some further connection be needed? Is the group of lines a' poem if "we" can make the connections? Is it a poem where no connection is

71

apparent to "us"? If the lines come in sequence on a single occasion does the unity of the occasion connect them into a single poem? Can many poems be a single poem as well? (They often are.)

What's a sequence anyway?

What's unity?

The Unity of "Primitive" Thought & Its Shattering

The anthology shows some ways in which the unity is achieved —in general by the imposition of some constant or "key" against which all disparate materials can be measured. A sound, a rhythm, a name, an image, a dream, a gesture, a picture, an action, a silence: any or all of these can function as "keys." Beyond that there's no need for consistency, for fixed or discrete meanings. An object is whatever it becomes under the impulse of the situation at hand. Forms are often open. Causality is often set aside. The poet (who may also be dancer, singer, magician, whatever the event demands of him) masters a series of techniques that can fuse the most seemingly contradictory propositions.

But above all there's a sense-of-unity that surrounds the poem, a reality concept that acts as a cement, a unification of perspective linking

poet & man
man & world
world & image
image & word
word & music
music & dance
dance & dancer
dancer & man
man & world
etc.

all of which has been put in many different ways—by Cassirer notably as a feeling for "the solidarity of all life" leading toward a "law of metamorphosis" in thought & word.

Within this undifferentiated & unified frame with its open images & mixed media, there are rarely "poems" as we know them—but we come in with our analytical minds & shatter the unity. It has in fact been shattered already by workers before us.

Primitive & Modern: Intersections & Analogies

Like any collector, my approach to delimiting & recognizing what's a poem has been by analogy: in this case (beyond the obvious definition of poems as words-of-songs) to the work of modern poets. Since much of this work has been revolutionary & limit-smashing, the analogy in turn expands the range of what "we" can see as primitive poetry. It also shows some of the ways in which primitive poetry & thought are close to an impulse toward unity in our own time, of which the poets are forerunners. The important intersections (analogies) are:

(1) the poem carried by the voice: a "pre"-literate situation of poetry composed to be spoken, chanted or, more accurately, sung; compare this to the "post-literate" situation, in McLuhan's good phrase, or where-we-are-today;

> written poem as score
> public readings
>
> poets' theaters
> jazz poetry
> rock poetry etc.

(2) a highly developed process of image-thinking: concrete or non-causal thought in contrast to the simplifications of Aristotelian logic, etc., with its "objective categories" & rules of non-contradiction; a "logic" of polarities; creation thru dream, etc.; modern poetry (having had & outlived the experience of rationalism) enters a post-logical phase;

> Blake's multi-images
> symbolism
> surrealism
>
> deep-image
>
> random poetry
> composition by field etc.

(3) a "minimal" art of maximal involvement; compound elements, each clearly articulated, & with plenty of room for fill-in (gaps in

> concrete poetry

sequence, etc.): the "spectator" as (ritual) participant who pulls it all together;

(4) an "intermedia" situation, as further denial of the categories: the poet's techniques aren't limited to verbal maneuvers but operate also through song, non-verbal sound, visual signs, & the varied activities of the ritual event: here the "poem" = the work of the "poet" in whatever medium, or (where we're able to grasp it) the totality of the work;

> picture poems
> prose poems
>
> happenings
> total theater
>
> poets as film-makers etc.

(5) the animal-body-rootedness of "primitive" poetry: recognition of a "physical" basis for the poem within a man's body—or as an act of body & mind together, breath &/or spirit; in many cases too the direct & open handling of sexual imagery & (in the "events") of sexual activities as key factors in creation of the sacred;

> dada
> lautgedichte (sound poems)
>
> beast language
>
> line & breath
> projective verse etc.
>
> sexual revolution etc.

(6) the poet as shaman, or primitive shaman as poet & seer thru control of the means just stated: an open "visionary" situation prior to all system-making ("priesthood") in which the man creates thru dream (image) & word (song), "that Reason may have ideas to build on" (W. Blake).

> Rimbaud's voyant
> Rilke's angel
> Lorca's duende
>
> beat poetry
> psychedelic see-in's, be-in's, etc.
>
> individual neo-shamanisms, etc., works directly influenced by the "other" poetry or by analogies to "primitive art": ideas of negritude, tribalism, wilderness, etc.

What's more, the translations themselves may create new forms & shapes-of-poems with their own energies & interest—another intersection that can't be overlooked.

74

In all this the ties feel very close—not that "we" & "they" are identical, but that the systems of thought & the poetry they've achieved are, like what we're after, distinct from something in the "West," & we can now see & value them because of it. What's missing are the in-context factors that define them more closely group-by-group: the sense of the poems as part of an integrated social & religious complex; the presence in each instance of specific myths & locales; the fullness of the living culture. Here the going is rougher with no easy shortcuts through translation: no simple carry-overs. If our world is open to multiple influences & data, theirs is largely self-contained. If we're committed to a search for the "new," most of them are tradition-bound. (The degree to which "they" are can be greatly exaggerated.) If the poet's purpose among us is "to spread doubt & create illusion" (N. Calas), among them it's to overcome it.

That they've done so *without denying the reality* is also worth remembering. . . .

TOTAL TRANSLATION: AN EXPERIMENT IN THE PRESENTATION OF AMERICAN INDIAN POETRY (1969)

It wasn't really a "problem," as these things are sometimes called, but to get closer to a way of poetry that had concerned me from years before, though until this project I'd only been able to approach it at a far remove. I'd been translating "tribal" poetry (the latest, still imperfect substitute I can find for "primitive," which continues to bother me) out of books: doing my versions from earlier translations into languages I could cope with, including English. Toward the end of my work on *Technicians* I met Stanley Diamond, anthropologist & friend of Gary Snyder's, who directed me to the Senecas in upstate New York, & David McAllester, ethnomusicologist at Wesleyan University, who showed me how a few songs worked in Navajo. With their help (& a nod from Dell Hymes as well) I later was able to get Wenner-Gren Foundation support to carry on a couple of experiments in the translation of American Indian poetry. I'm far enough into them by now to say a little about what I've been doing.

•

In the summer of 1968 I began to work simultaneously with two sources of Indian poetry. Settling down a mile from the Cold Spring settlement of the Allegany (Seneca) Reservation at Steamburg, New York, I was near enough to friends who were traditional songmen to work with them on the translation of sacred & secular song-poems. At the same time David McAllester was sending me recordings, transcriptions, literal translations & his own freer reworkings of a series of seventeen "horse songs" that had been the property of Frank Mitchell, a Navajo singer from Chinle, Arizona (born: 1881, died: 1967). Particularly with the Senecas (where I didn't know in the first instance what, if anything, I was going to get) my first concern was with the translation process itself. While I'll limit myself to that right now, I should at least say (things never seem to be clear unless you say them) that if I hadn't also come up with matter that I could "internalize," I would have floundered long before this.

The big question, which I was immediately aware of with both poetries, was if & how to handle those elements in the original works that weren't translatable literally. As with most Indian poetry, the voice carried many sounds that weren't, strictly speaking, "words." These tended to disappear or be attentuated in translation, as if they weren't really there. But they *were* there & were at least as important as the words themselves. In both Navajo & Seneca many songs consisted of nothing but those "meaningless" vocables (not free "scat" either but fixed sounds recurring from performance to performance). Most other songs had both meaningful & non-meaningful elements, & such songs (McAllester told me for the Navajo) were often spoken of, qua title, by their meaningless burdens. Similar meaningless sounds, Dell Hymes had pointed out for some Kwakiutl songs, might in fact be keys to the songs' structures: "something usually disregarded, the refrain or so-called 'nonsense syllables' . . . in fact of fundamental importance . . . both structural clue & microcosm."

So there were all these indications that the exploration of "pure sound" wasn't beside the point of those poetries but at or near their heart: all of this coincidental too with concern for the sound-poem among a number of modern poets. Accepting its meaningfulness here, I more easily accepted it there. I also realized (with the Navajo especially) that there were more than simple refrains involved: that we, as translators & poets, had been taking a rich *oral* poetry & translating it to be read primarily for meaning, thus denuding it to say the least.

Here's an immediate example of what I mean. In the first of Frank Mitchell's seventeen horse-songs, the opening line comes out as follows in McAllester's transcription:

dzo-wowode sileye shi, dza-na desileye shiyi, dzanadi sileye
    shiya'e

but the same segment given "as spoken" reads:

dzą́ądi silá shi dzą́ądi silá shi dzą́ądi silá shi

which translates as "over-here it-is-there (&) mine" repeated three times. So does the line as sung if all you're accounting for is the meaning. In other words, translate only for meaning & you get the three-fold repetition of an unchanging single statement; but in the Navajo each time it's delivered there's a sharp departure from the spoken form: thus three distinct sound-events, not one-in-triplicate!

I know neither Navajo nor Seneca except for bits of information picked up from grammar books & such (also the usual social fall-out among the Senecas: "cat," "dog," "thank you," "you're welcome," numbers one to ten, "uncle," "father," & my Indian name). But even from this far away, I can (with a little help from my friends) be aware of my options as translator. Let me try, then, to respond to *all* the sounds I'm made aware of, to let that awareness touch off responses or events in the English. I don't want to set English words to Indian music, but to respond poem-for-poem in the attempt to work out a "total" translation—not only of the words but of all sounds connected with the poem, including finally the music itself.

•

Seneca & Navajo are very different worlds, & what's an exciting procedure for one may be deadening or irrelevant for the other. The English translation should match the character of the Indian original: take that as a goal & don't worry about how literal you're otherwise being. Walter Lowenfels calls poetry "the continuation of journalism by other means," & maybe that holds too for translation-as-poem. I translate, then, as a way of reporting what I've sensed or seen of an other's situation: true as far as possible to "my" image of the life & thought of the source.

Living with the Senecas helped in that sense. I don't know how much stress to put on this, but I know that in so far as I developed a strategy for translation from Seneca, I tried to keep to approaches I felt were consistent with their life-style. I can hardly speak of the poetry without using words that would describe the people as well. Not that it's easy to sum up any people's poetry or its frame-of-mind, but since one is always doing it in translation, I'll attempt it also by way of description.

Seneca poetry, when it uses words at all, works in sets of short songs, minimal realizations colliding with each other in marvelous ways, a very light, very pointed play-of-the-mind, nearly always just a step away from the comic (even as their masks are), the words set out in clear relief against the ground of the ("meaningless") refrain. Clowns stomp & grunt through the longhouse, but in subtler ways too the encouragement to "play" is always a presence. Said the leader of the longhouse religion at Allegany, explaining why the seasonal ceremonies ended with a gambling game: the idea of a religion was to reflect the *total* order of the universe while providing an outlet for *all* human needs, the need for play not least among them. Although it pretty clearly doesn't work out as well nowadays as that makes it sound—the orgiastic past & the "doings" (happenings) in which men were free to live out their dreams dimming from generation to generation—still the resonance, the ancestral permissiveness, keeps being felt in many ways. Sacred occasions may be serious & necessary, but it doesn't take much for the silence to be broken by laughter: thus, says Richard Johnny John, if you call for a medicine ceremony of the mystic animals & it turns out that no one's sick & in need of curing, the head-one tells the others: "I leave it up to you folks & if you want to have a good time, have a good time!" He knows they will anyway.

I take all of that as cue: to let my moves be directed by a sense of the songs & of the attitudes surrounding them. Another thing I try not to overlook is that the singers & I, while separated in Seneca, are joined in English. That they have to translate for me is a problem at first, but the problem suggests its own solution. Since they're bilingual, sometimes beautifully so, why not work from that instead of trying to get around it? Their English, fluent while identifiably Senecan, is as much a commentary on where they are as mine is on where I am. Given the "minimal" nature of much of the poetry (one of its *strongest* features, in fact) there's no need for a dense response in English. Instead I can leave myself free to structure the final poem by using their English as a base: a particular enough form of the language to itself be an extra means for the extension of reportage through poetry & translation.

I end up collaborating & happy to do so, since translation (maybe poetry as well) has always involved that kind of thing for me. The collaboration can take a number of forms. At one extreme I have only to make it possible for the other man to take over: in this case, to set up or simply to encourage a situation in which a man who's never thought of himself as a "poet" can begin to structure his utterances with a care for phrasing & spacing that drives them toward poetry. *Example:* Dick Johnny John & I had taped his Seneca version of the thanking prayer that opens all longhouse gatherings & were translating it phrase by phrase. He had decided to write it down himself, to give the translation to his sons, who from oldest to youngest were progressively losing the Seneca language. I could follow his script from where I sat, & the method of punctuation he was using seemed special to me, since in letters & such he punctuates more or less conventionally. Anyway, I got his punctuation down along with his wording, with which he was taking a lot of time both in response to my questions & from his desire "to word it just the way it says there." In setting up the result, I let the periods in his prose version mark the ends of lines, made some vocabulary choices that we'd left hanging, & tried for the rest to keep clear of what was after all his poem. Later I titled it *Thank You: A Poem in 17 Parts,* & wrote a note on it for *El Corno Emplumado,** where it was printed in English & Spanish. This is the first of the seventeen sections:

Now so many people that are in this place.
In our meeting place.
It starts when two people see each other.
They greet each other.
Now we greet each other.
Now he thought.
I will make the Earth where some people can walk around.

* Magazine edited & published by Sergio Mondragón & Margaret Randall in Mexico City.

I have created them, now this has happened.
We are walking on it.
Now this time of the day.
We give thanks to the Earth.
This is the way it should be in our minds.

[*Note:* The set-up in English doesn't, as far as I can tell, reproduce the movement of the Seneca text. More interestingly it's itself a consideration of that movement: is in fact Johnny John's reflections upon the values, the relative strengths of elements in his text. The poet is to a great degree concerned with what-stands-out & where, & his phrasing reveals it, no less here than in any other poem.]

Even when being more active myself, I would often defer to others in the choice of words. Take, for example, a set of seven Woman's Dance songs with words, composed by Avery Jimerson & translated with help from his wife, Fidelia. Here the procedure was for Avery to record the song, for Fidelia to paraphrase it in English, then for the three of us to work out a transcription & word-by-word translation by a process of question & answer. Only afterward would I actively come into it, to try to work out a poem in English with enough swing to it to return more or less to the area of song. *Example:* The paraphrase of the 6th Song reads:

Very nice, nice, when our mothers do the ladies' dance.
Graceful, nice, very nice, when our mothers do the ladies' dance . . .

while the word-by-word, including the "meaningless" refrain, reads:

hey heyah yo oh ho
nice nice nice-it-is
when-they-dance-the-ladies-dance
our-mothers
gahnoweyah heyah
graceful it-is
nice nice nice-it-is
when-they-dance-the-ladies-dance
our-mothers
gahnoweyah heyah (& repeat).

In doing *these* songs, I decided in fact to translate for meaning, since the meaningless vocables used by Jimerson were only the standard markers that turn up in all the woman's songs: *hey heyah yo* to mark the opening, *gahnoweyah heyah* to mark the internal transitions. (In my translation, I sometimes use a simple "hey," "oh" or "yeah" as a rough equivalent, but let the movement of the English determine its position.) I also decided not to fit English words to Jimerson's melody, regarding that as a kind of oil-&-water treatment, but to suggest (as with most of our own poetry) a music through the normally pitched speaking voice. For the rest I was following Fidelia Jimerson's lead:

hey it's nice it's nice it's nice
to see them yeah to see
our mothers do the ladies' dances
oh it's graceful & it's
nice it's nice it's very nice
to see them hey to see
our mothers do the ladies' dances.

With other kinds of song-poems I would also, as often as not, stick close to the translation-as-given, departing from that to better get the point of the whole across in English, to normalize the word order where phrases in the literal translation appeared in their original Seneca sequence, or to get into the play-of-the-thing on my own. The most important group of songs I was working on was a sacred cycle called *Idos* (ee-dos) in Seneca—in English either *Shaking the Pumpkin* or, more ornately, *The Society of the Mystic Animals*. Like most Seneca songs *with* words (most Seneca songs are in fact *without* words), the typical Pumpkin song contains a single statement, or a single statement alternating with a row of vocables, which is repeated anywhere from three to six or seven times. Some songs are nearly identical with some others (same melody & vocables, slight change in words) but aren't necessarily sung in sequence. In a major portion of the ceremony, in fact, a fixed order for the songs is completely abandoned, & each person present takes a turn at singing a ceremonial (medicine) song of his own choice. There's room here too for messing around.

Richard Johnny John was my collaborator on the Pumpkin songs, & the basic wording is therefore his. My intention was to account for all vocal sounds in the original but—as a more "interesting" way of handling the minimal structures & allowing a very clear, very pointed emergence of perceptions—to translate the poems *onto the page,* as with "concrete" or other types of minimal poetry. Where several songs showed a concurrence of structure, I allowed myself the option of treating them individually or combining them into one. I've deferred singing until some future occasion.

Take the opening songs of the ceremony. These are fixed pieces sung by the ceremonial leader *(hajaswas)* before he throws the meeting open to the individual singers. The melody & structure of the first nine are identical: very slow, a single line of words ending with a string of sounds, etc., the pattern identical until the last go-round, when the song ends with a grunting expulsion of breath into a weary "ugh" sound. I had to get all of that across: the bareness, the regularity, the deliberateness of the song, along with the basic meaning, repeated vocables, emphatic terminal sound, & (still following Johnny John's reminder to play around with it "if everything's all right") a little something of my own. The song whose repeated line is:

> The animals are coming by *heh eh heh* (or *heh eh-eh-eh heh*)

can then become:

```
T                                H  E  H  E  H  H  E  H
h
e                                H  E  H  E  H  H  E  H

The animals are coming by  H  E  H  U  H  H  E  H
n
i                                H  E  H  E  H  H  E  H
m
a                                H  E  H  E  H  H  E  H
l
s
```

& the next one:

T		H	E	H	E	H	H	E	H
h									
e		H	E	H	E	H	H	E	H
The doings were beginning		H	E	H	**U**	**H**	H	E	H
o									
i		H	E	H	E	H	H	E	H
n		H	E	H	E	H	H	E	H
g									
s									

& so forth: each poem set, if possible, on its own page, as further analogue to the slowness, the deliberate pacing of the original.

The use of vertical titles is the only move I make without immediate reference to the Seneca version: the rest I'd feel to be programmed by elements in the original prominent enough for me to respond to in the movement from oral to visual structure. Where the song comes without vocables, I don't supply them but concentrate on presentation of the words. Thus in two groups of "crow songs," one's a simple translation-for-meaning; the other ("in the manner of Zukofsky") puns off the Seneca sound:

> yehgagaweeyo (*lit. that pretty crow*) becomes "yond caw-crow's way-out"

&

> hongyasswahyaenee *(lit. that [pig]-meat's for me)* becomes "Hog (yes!) swine you're mine"

while trying at the same time to let something of the meaning come through.

A motive behind the punning was, I suppose, the desire to bring across (i.e., "translate") the feeling of the Seneca word for crow (*gaga* or *kaga*), which is at the same time an imitation of the bird's voice. In another group—three songs about the owl—I pick up the vocables suggesting the animal's call & shape them into an outline of a giant owl, within which frame the poems are printed. But that's only where the mimicry of the original is strong enough to trigger an equivalent move in translation; otherwise my inclination is to *present* analogues to the full range of vocal sound, etc., but not to *represent* the poem's subject as "mere picture."

The variety of possible moves is obviously related to the variety—semantic & aural—of the cycle itself.*

[*Note*. Behind it all there's a hidden motive too: not simply to make clear the world of the original, but to do so at some remove from the song itself: to reflect the song without the "danger" of presenting any part of it (the melody, say) exactly as given: thus to have it while not having it, in deference to the sense of secrecy & localization that's so important to those for whom the songs are sacred & alive. So the changes resulting from translation are, in this instance, not only inevitable but desired, or, as another Seneca said to me: "We wouldn't want the songs to get so far away from us; no, the songs would be too lonely."]

•

My decision with the Navajo horse songs was to work with the sound as sound: a reflection in itself of the difference between Navajo & Seneca song structure. For Navajo (as already indicated) is much fuller, much denser, twists words into new shapes or fills up the spaces between words by insertion of a wide range of "meaningless" vocables, making it misleading to translate primarily for meaning or, finally, to think of *total* translation in any terms but those of sound. Look, for example, at the number of free vocables in the following excerpt from McAllester's relatively literal translation of the 16th Horse Song:

(nana na) Sun-(yeye ye) Standing-within (neye ye) Boy

    (Hehe ye) truly his horses
    ('Eye ye) abalone horses
    ('Eye ye) made of sunrays
    (Neye ye) their bridles

    (Gowo wo) coming on my right side
    (Jeye yeye) coming into my hand (yeye neyowo 'ei).

* For which see the author's complete version in *Shaking the Pumpkin* (Doubleday, 1972).

Now this, which even so doesn't show the additional word distortions that turn up in the singing, might be brought closer to English word order & translated for meaning alone as something like

Boy who stands inside the Sun
with your horses that are
abalone horses
bridles
made of sunrays
rising on my right side
coming to my hand
etc.

But what a difference from the fantastic way the sounds cut through the words & between them from the first line of the original on.

It was the possibility of working with all that sound, finding my own way into it in English, that attracted me now—that & a quality in Mitchell's voice I found irresistible. It was, I think, that the music was so clearly within range of the language: it was song & it was poetry, & it seemed possible at least that the song issued from the poetry, was an extension of it or rose inevitably from the juncture of words & other vocal sounds. So many of us had already become interested in this kind of thing as poets, that it seemed natural to me to be in a situation where the poetry would be leading me toward a (new) music *it* was generating.

I began with the 10th Horse Song, which had been the first one Mitchell sang when McAllester was recording him. At that point I didn't know if I'd do much more than quote or allude to the vocables: possibly pull them or something like them into the English. I was *writing* at first, working on the words by sketching-in phrases that seemed natural to my own sense of the language. In the 10th Song there's a division of speakers: the main voice is that of Enemy Slayer or Dawn Boy, who first brought horses to The People, but the chorus is sung by his father, the Sun, telling him to take spirit horses & other precious animals & goods to the house of his mother, Changing

Woman. The literal translation of the refrain— (*to*) *the woman, my son*—seemed a step away from how we'd say it, though normal enough in Navajo. It was with the sense that, whatever distortions in sound the Navajo showed, the syntax was natural, that I changed McAllester's suggested reading to *go to her my son,* & his opening line

Boy-brought-up-within-the-Dawn It is I, I who am that one

(lit. *being that one,* with a suggestion of causation), to

Because I was the boy raised in the dawn.

At the same time I was, I thought, getting it down to more or less the economy of phrasing of the original.

I went through the first seven or eight lines like that but still hadn't gotten to the vocables. McAllester's more "factual" approach—reproducing the vocables exactly—seemed wrong to me on one major count. In the Navajo the vocables give a very clear sense of continuity from the verbal material; i.e., the vowels in particular show a rhyming or assonantal relationship between the "meaningless" & meaningful segments:

'Esdza shiye'	e hye-la	'esdza shiye'	e hye-la naŋa yeye 'e
The woman,	*(voc.)*	*The woman,*	*(voc.)*
my son		*my son*	

whereas the English words for this & many other situations in the poem are, by contrast to the Navajo, more rounded & further back in the mouth. Putting the English words ("son" here but "dawn," "home," "upon," "blown," etc. further on) against the Navajo vocables (*e hye-la naŋa yeye 'e,* etc.) denies the musical coherence of the original & destroys the actual flow.

I decided to *translate* the vocables, & from that point was already playing with the possibility of *translating* other elements in the songs not usually handled by translation. It also seemed important to get as far away as I could from *writing.* So I began to speak, then sing my own words over Mitchell's tape, replacing his vocables with sounds relevant to me, then putting my version on a fresh tape, having now to work it in

87

its own terms. It wasn't an easy thing either for me to break the silence or go beyond the shallow pitch levels of my speaking voice, & I was still finding it more natural in that early version to replace the vocables with small English words (it's hard for a word-poet to lose words completely), hoping some of their semantic force would lessen with reiteration:

Go to her my son *& one &* go to her my son *& one & one & none & gone*

Go to her my son *& one &* go to her my son *& one & one & none & gone*

Because I was the boy raised in the dawn *& one &* go to her my son *& one & one & none & gone*

& leaving from the house the bluestone home *& one &* go to her my son *& one & one & none & gone*

& leaving from the house the shining home *& one &* go to her my son *& one & one & none &gone*

& from the swollen house my breath has blown *& one &* go to her my son *& one & one & none & gone*

& so on. In the transference too—likely enough because my ear is so damn slow—I found I was considerably altering Mitchell's melody; but really that was part of the translation process also: a change responsive to the translated sounds & words I was developing.

In singing the 10th Song I was able to bring the small words (vocable substitutions) even further into the area of pure vocal sound (the difference, if it's clear from the spelling, between *one, none* & *gone* and *wnn, nnnn* & *gahn*): soundings that would carry into the other songs at an even greater remove from the discarded meanings:

Because I was thnboyngnng raised ing the dawn NwnnN go to her my son N wnn N wnn N nnnn N gahn
Etcetera.

What I was doing in one sense was contributing & then obliterating my own level of meaning, while in another sense it was as if I was recapitulating the history of the vocables themselves, at least according to one of the standard explanations that sees them as remnants of archaic words that have been emptied of meaning: a process I could still sense elsewhere in the Horse Songs—for example, where the sound *howo* turns up as both a "meaningless" vocable & a distorted form of the word *hoghan* = house. But even if I was doing something like that in an accelerated way, that wasn't the real point of it for me. Rather what I was getting at was the establishment of a series of sounds that were assonant with the range of my own vocabulary in the translation, & to which I could refer whenever the Navajo sounds for which they were substitutes turned up in Mitchell's songs.

In spite of carry-overs, these basic soundings were different for each song (more specifically, for each *pair* of songs), & I found, as I moved from one song to another, that I had to establish my sound equivalencies before going into the actual translations. For this I made use of the traditional way the Navajo songs begin: with a short string of vocables that will be picked up (in whole or in part) as the recurring burden of the song. I found I could set most of my basic vocables or vocable-substitutes into the opening, using it as a key to which I could refer when necessary to determine sound substitutions, not only for the vocables but for word distortions in the meaningful segments of the poems. There was a cumulative effect here too. The English vocabulary of the 10th Song— strong on back vowels, semivowels, glides & nasals—influenced the choice of vocables: the vocables influenced further vocabulary choices & vocables in the other songs. (*Note*: The vocabulary of many of the songs is very close to begin with, the most significant differences in "pairs" of songs coming from the alternation of blue & white color symbolism.) Finally, the choice of sounds influenced the style of my singing by setting up a great deal of resonance I found I could control to serve as a kind of drone behind my voice. In ways like this the translation was assuming a life of its own.

With the word distortions too, it seemed to me that the most I should do was approximate the degree of distortion in the original. McAllester had provided two Navajo texts—the words as sung & as they would be if spoken—& I aimed at roughly the amount of variation I could discern between the two. I further assumed that every perceivable change was significant, & there were indications in fact of a surprising degree of precision in Mitchell's delivery, where even what seem to be false steps or accidents may really be gestures to intensify the special or sacred powers of the song at the points in question. Songs 10 & 11, for example, are structurally paired, & in both songs Mitchell seems to be fumbling at the beginning of the 21st line after the opening choruses. Maybe it was accidental & maybe not, but I figured I might as well go wrong by overdoing the distortion, here & wherever else I had the choice.

So I followed where Mitchell led me, responding to all moves of his I was aware of & letting them program or initiate the moves I made in translation. All of this within obvious limits: those imposed by the field of sound I was developing in English. . . . Throughout the songs I've now been into, I've worked in pretty much that way: the relative densities determined by the original, the final form by the necessities of the poem as it took shape for me. Obviously, too, there were larger patterns to keep in mind, when a particular variation occurred in a series of positions, etc. To say any more about that—though the approach changed in the later songs I worked on, toward a more systematic handling—would be to put greater emphasis on method than any poem can bear. More important for me was actually being in the stimulus & response situation, certainly the most *physical* translation I've ever been involved in. I hope that that much comes through for anyone who hears these sung.

But there was still another step I had to take. While the tape I was working from was of Mitchell singing by himself, in actual performance he would likely be accompanied by all those present with him at the blessing. The typical Navajo performance pattern, as McAllester described it to me, calls for each person present to follow the singer to whatever degree he can. The result is highly individualized singing (only the ceremonial singer is likely to know all of it the right way) & leads to an actual indeterminacy of performance. Those who can't follow the words at all may make up their own vocal sounds—anything, in effect, for the sake of participation.

I saw the indeterminacy, etc., as key to the further extension of the poems into the area of total translation & total performance. (Instrumentation & ritual-events would be further "translation" possibilities, but the Horse Songs are rare among Navajo poems in not including them.) To work out the extension for multiple voices, I again made use of the tape recorder, this time of a four-track system on which I laid down the following as typical of the possibilities at hand:

TRACK ONE. A clean recording of the lead voice.

TRACK TWO. A voice responsive to the first but showing less word distortion & occasional free departures from the text.

TRACK THREE. A voice limited to pure-sound improvisations on the meaningless elements in the text.

TRACK FOUR. A voice similar to that on the second track but distorted by means of a violin amplifier placed against the throat & set at "echo" or "tremolo." To be used only as a barely audible background filler for the others.

Once the four tracks were recorded (I've only done it so far for the 12th Song), I had them balanced & mixed onto a monaural tape. In that way I could present the poems as I'd conceived them & as poetry in fact had always existed for men like Mitchell—to be heard without reference to their incidental appearance on the page.*

●

Translation is carry-over. It is a means of delivery & of bringing to life. It begins with a forced change of language, but a change too that opens up the possibility of greater understanding. Everything in these song-poems is finally translatable: words, sounds, voice, melody, gesture, event, etc., in the reconstitution of a unity that would be shattered by approaching each element in isolation. A full & total experience begins it, which only a total translation can fully bring across.

* A later, significantly different tape version was published as *6 Horse Songs for 4 Voices* (New Wilderness Audiographics, New York, 1978).

By saying which, I'm not trying to coerce anyone (least of all myself) with the idea of a single relevant approach to translation. I'll continue, I believe, to translate in part or in any other way I feel moved to; nor would I deny the value of handling words or music or events as separate phenomena. It's possible too that a prose description of the song-poems, etc. might tell pretty much what was happening in & around them, but no amount of description can provide the *immediate* perception translation can. One way or another translation makes a poem in this place that's analogous in whole or in part to a poem in that place. The more the translator can perceive of the original—not only the language but, more basically perhaps, the living situation from which it comes &, very much so, the living voice of the singer—the more of it he should be able to deliver. In the same process he will be presenting something—i.e., making something present, or making something as a present—for his own time & place.

Stony Brook, Number 3–4, Autumn 1969.

PRE-FACE II:
SHAKING THE PUMPKIN (1972)

> "Come not thus with your gunnes & swords, to invade as foes . . .
>
> "What will it availe you to take that perforce you may quietly have with love, or to destroy them that provide your food? . . .
>
> "Lie well, & sleepe quietly with my women & children, laugh, & I will be merrie with you. . . ."
>
> —POWHATAN, *to Capt. John Smith*

1.

The awkwardness of presenting translations from American Indian poetry in the year 1972 is that it has become fashionable today to deny the possibility of crossing the boundaries that separate people of different races & cultures: to insist instead that black is the concern of black, red of red, & white of white. Yet the idea of translation has always been that such boundary crossing is not only possible but desirable. By its very nature, translation asserts or at least implies a concept of psychic & biological unity, weird as such assertion may seem in a time of growing dis-integration. Each poem, being made present & translated, flies in the face of divisive ideology. The question for the translator is not whether but how far we can translate one another. Like the poet who is his brother, he attempts to restore what has been torn apart. Any arrogance on his part would not only lead to paternalism or "colonialism" (LeRoi Jones's term for it from a few years back), it would deny the very order of translation. Only if he allows himself to be directed by the other will a common way emerge, true to both positions.

To submit through translation is to begin to accept the "truths" of an other's language. At the same time it's a way of growing wary of the lies in one's own, a point of vigilance that translators & poets should be particularly keyed to. I learned, for example, that the Senecas with whom I lived call the whites "younger brothers" & themselves "*real* people." To understand the Seneca experience (including where I stand with relation to them) I have to submit to terms like these & to get to a truth about them which includes the Seneca truth. As I do, it becomes clear to me that the very nature of "Indian" & "white" (words basic to the process I'm describing) is itself a question of language & translation.

If the term "younger brother" would later be neutralized or come to suggest contempt, what relationship did it originally express in a culture that didn't practice primogeniture & individual ownership of land—in which forest & clearings (the men were hunters, the women gardeners) were a common ground for brothers as children of one mother & members of one clan? Whether by birth or adoption didn't matter either: descended from a single mother (ultimately the Earth), "older" & "younger" was for them a matter of precedence in time & place, their relative experience of the shared environment. Thus the Senecas as older brothers recognized the rights of both to start with, but the whites (children also of the "old world" patriarchy) came to the land prepared for dispossession & fratricide. In the overthrow of the older—refusing adoption to the real-personhood of the Indian way, while asserting their own great-white-fatherhood—they triggered a disruption of the natural (ecological) order that's now making all of us its victims.

A "real" person in these terms is one who hasn't forgotten what & where things are in relation to the Earth. Earth-rooted, he is royal too, not by precedence of birth, but insofar as he has & shares a knowledge of the realm. He has only to maintain a true eye for his surroundings & a contact with the Earth, to recognize himself as the inheritor of reality, of a more real way of life. At any rate that seems to be the claim implicit in the language & confirmed by the events that have followed its denial.

The issue, writes David Antin, is reality. The *real* person (reality-person, in fact) lives, like the "primitive" philosopher described by Radin, "in a blaze of reality" through which he can experience "reality at white heat." This is a part of the tribal inheritance (not Indian only but world-wide) that we all lose at our peril—younger & older alike. Remember too how many elements are active in that situation, where we would concentrate on the words as being particularly the "poem" (many Indian poems in fact dispense entirely with words): elements, I mean, like music, non-verbal phonetic sounds, dance, gesture & event, game, dream, etc., along with all those unstated ideas & images the participants pick up from the poem's context. Each moment is charged: each is a point at which meaning is coming to surface, where nothing's incidental but everything matters terribly.

Now, put all of that together & you have the makings of a high poetry & art, which only a colonialist ideology could have blinded us into labeling "primitive" or "savage." You have also the great hidden accomplishment of our older brothers in America, made clear in the poetry & yet of concern not only to poets but to all (red, white & black) who want to carry the possibilities of reality & personhood into any new worlds to come. The yearning to rediscover the Red Man is part of this. It acknowledges not only the cruelty of what's happening in this place (a negative matter of genocide & guilt) but leads as well to the realization that "we" in a larger sense will never be whole without a recovery of the "red power" that's been here from the beginning. The true integration must begin & end with a recognition of all such powers. That means a process of translation & of mutual completion. Not a brotherhood of lies this time but an affiliation based on what the older had known from the start: that we're doomed without his tribal & matrilocal wisdom, which can be shared only among equals who have recognized a common lineage from the Earth.

2.

The question, then, was how to deliver the poetry of the first discoverers of America & civilizers of themselves. I had previously been retranslating (I wasn't unique in this among

American poets) & anthologizing Indian & other tribal &/or "primitive" poetries mostly from the abundant volumes of myths & texts gathered over the previous hundred or so years by scores of Boasian anthropologists & others. That work resulted in *Technicians of the Sacred,* which included, in addition to my own contributions, workings by such poets as Pound, Williams, Tzara, Waley, Merwin, Sanders, Kelly, & R. Owens, plus very solid translations by anthropologists, etc. like Densmore, Berndt, Quain, Matthews, Bleek & Lloyd, McAllester, Beier, & many others. Not to mention all the workers (some better known than these) whose gatherings from around-the-world served as sources for the poems that emerged in English.

There are a couple of points from *Technicians* that I want to reiterate here. First it seemed clear to me that the range-&-depth of the materials previously collected was astonishing, & that the levels of the poetry were in no obvious relationship to the economic or industrial development of the cultures from which they derived (or if they were, that the powers of the poetry declined as those of technology & the political state increased)—clear, I mean, in spite of considerable mistranslation in even the "literal" & interlinear texts, & the fact that many of the translated poems were practically unreadable as first presented. Second, the range of the tribal poets was even more impressive if one avoided a closed, European definition of "poem" & worked empirically or by analogy to contemporary, limit-smashing experiments (as with concrete poetry, sound poetry, intermedia, happenings, etc.) Since tribal poetry was almost always part of a larger situation (i.e. was truly intermedia), there was no more reason to present the words alone as independent structures than the ritual-events, say, or the pictographs arising from the same source. Where possible, in fact, one might present or translate all elements connected with the total "poem"—a concern that continues into the present book. . . .

Unlike *Technicians* this gathering is almost completely a poet's book, & that in itself is an important step toward the larger work of translation & recovery I'd been hoping to develop. Several included herein had already been working in this area: W. S. Merwin for at least the previous decade but with more recent emphasis on Plains Indian texts out of Lowie; Edward Field going the length of a book of adaptations from Rasmussen's Eskimo collections; Carl Cary working from anthropological texts & also from his earlier Skagit contacts; & James Koller naturalizing works from Tlingit & Sioux toward an immediate grasp of some of the levels of vision they represent. Some others responded directly to my request for help—Armand Schwerner, Stephen Berg, & Anselm Hollo with greatest energy; Nathaniel Tarn equally so, but bringing to it also a considerable personal acquaintance with the contemporary Mayans of Guatemala—working from earlier translations into French, Spanish & German, or from English versions that had failed to match the life of their sources. But new works by anthropologists were important too, especially where they disclosed actual structural possibilities or ways of showing those in translation: Dennis Tedlock's total translations of Zuni narratives, say, which forever did away with the idea that "prose" could be the medium of a spoken narrative, or Munro Edmonson's verse reconstruction of the *Popol Vuh*. To say nothing of McAllester's Navajo Horse Songs, which were the solid basis for whatever workings I was then able to perform.

In each case the translator's voice is very different—which is the way it should be. For the translator—if he's to match the interest of the original—must extend its meanings into his own language & by means of his own voice. (This assumes a poet's voice to begin with.) He needn't lose his personhood but may extend that too & make it real—in translation as well as in any of his other workings. This has always been the way of the great poet-translators—Catullus or Chaucer or Marpa or Pound—& its beginnings here may hopefully mark the real emergence of Indian poetry into the consciousness of the non-Indian world.

Hopefully too it may coincide with Indian efforts to hold, to expand or (for many) to return to the sources of their own power—even to understand that power as not only particular to its immediate place-of-origin, but as part of an historically proven & worldwide manifestation of such poetic & trans-poetic powers. . . .

Nothing changes from generation to generation
except the thing seen
and that makes a composition.
—G. STEIN

PRE-FACE III:
REVOLUTION OF THE WORD
(1974)

1.
Autobiography

It was 1948 & by year's end I was seventeen. I had been coming into poetry for two years. My head was filled with Stein & Cummings, later with Williams, Pound, the French Surrealists, the Dada poets who made "pure sound" three decades earlier. Blues. American Indian things from Densmore. Cathay. Bible, Shakespeare, Whitman. Jewish liturgies. Dali & Lorca were ferocious possibilities. Joyce was incredible to any of our first sightings of his work. The thing was to get off on it, to hear one's mind, learn one's own voice. But the message clear & simple was to move. To change. To create one's self & thus one's poetry. A process.

But all that was from the vantage of where I had grown up, a little behind the times, in the Bronx of depression & World War II. To us the news hadn't yet filtered that the age of the modern, the experimental & visionary (for we sensed it even then as vision), had passed: to be replaced by a return to the old forms, to conventional metrics, diction, a responsible modernism, liberal & reformist, rational & refined, & goodbye to the madmen of language. Those were the first lessons of college days. They called it Auden or Lowell, Tate or Wilbur. Middle ground, like the politics then emerging. It became a question of amelioration. A shift of stance. A little toughening of Tennyson. Change the topic, the conversation. Change the footnotes. Kierkegaard instead of Darwin. Church instead of Nature. But the body of the poem must stay untouched. A virgin. The words must stay untouched. The images must be inherited & the inheritance must be along the line of what was called the "great tradition." Western. Christian. White.

I am trying to reconstruct, too sketchily, a sense of how all of that impinged: & how, because it impinged so much, it was possible, inevitable, that one saw the migration of modernism into the desert of the "New Critics" as the way (*the* way) it actually had happened. A few years later, poets of my generation would again break through, but rarely would we challenge the notion that there had been a virtual break in the continuity of avant-garde concerns. Rarely would we insist enough that the development of our own traditions had gone on uninterruptedly from their first eruption circa 1914 to their second in the 1950s. And if we said it, pointed out the irrelevance of the academic middle-grounders or resurrected the work of a (token) handful of survivors, the histories & anthologies were slower to respond & tell our story.

So I must sketch the other account first, the way it continues to be told among the academics: then give a sense of how we found our way to new views of our own immediate pre-history, & what aspects of those views this anthology is trying to present. For we are all, in different ways & from our individual perspectives, talking about a virtual revolution in consciousness, & if we can't remember how we got here, we may be talked into denying where we want to go.

2.
The Way We Learned Our History

1945–1950. World War II was over, & American poetry (what was then visible of the iceberg) had entered a strange condition. Something called "modern" was taken as an established fact, but so described as to presume a built-in self-destruct system that was already operative in the work of the inheritors. Wrote one of them, Delmore Schwartz: ". . . the poetic revolution, the revolution in poetic taste which was inspired by the criticism of T. S. Eliot . . . has established itself in power." And he gave as an example of new poets writing in "a style which takes as its starting point the poetic idiom and literary taste of the generation of Pound and Eliot," the following from W. D. Snodgrass:

The green catalpa tree has turned
All white; the cherry blooms once more.
In one whole year I haven't learned
A blessed thing they pay you for

—at which David Antin looks back & comments (1972): "The comparison of this updated version of *A Shropshire Lad* . . . and the poetry of the *Cantos* or *The Waste Land* seems so aberrant as to verge on the pathological."

Yet it was typical. Inevitable in fact for those who couldn't distinguish between "the poetic revolution" & a "revolution in taste," or who still thought of taste as an issue. Even an attempt at such distinctions was then unlikely, for the careers of the inheritors were too often "literary," resting like the idea of literature itself on a fixed notion of poetry & poem, which might be improved upon but never questioned *at the root.* And behind it too there was a strange fear of "freedom" as that had been articulated by earlier moderns—whether as "free verse" or "free love" or the abandonment of judgment as a bind on the intelligence or of taste as a determinant of value. So if the taste & judgment they still clung to (& which made them poets "inspired by the criticism of T. S. Eliot") demanded "modern" as an article of twentieth-century faith, they retained it; but they pulled back into traditional & institutional securities, "picking up again the meters" (Schwartz) as a moral buttress against their own despair. And this itself, qua ideology, was seen as part of a *modern* dilemma, which came to define their modern-ism, not as the promise of a new consciousness but as a glorified "failure of nerve."

Something of that sort must have been in Williams's mind when he spoke of *The Waste Land* as the "great catastrophe to our letters"—the one poetic event strong enough to draw numbers of the young back to the academic & conventional & to slow the momentum of the 1920s' avant-garde. The pullback, anyway, was explicit in Eliot's criticism & the late Tudor verse style of his shorter poems. But it was lurking as well in Pound's & Williams' own discomfort over *free* verse ("the magnificent failure of Walt Whitman"—W.C.W.) & in the need of many in their generation (almost an American obsession) to lay claim to Old World & "Anglo-Saxon" culture. In the 1920s it appeared in the high rhetoric of Hart Crane's verse—& in his sense that "the rebellion against . . . the so-called classical strictures" had ended—& it spawned the Southern Fugitives ("the only literary movement to begin in a frat house"—K. Rexroth), who pulled the verse back even further, while developing the concept of the new poet-critic.

If that was the line of descent that Schwartz found "taken for granted not only in poetry & the criticism of poetry, but in the teaching of literature" (1958), it's still worth giving in some detail because it has remained the going view of "modern" American poetry between the two world wars. Any such view has to be selective in its construction of the past. Those like Schwartz's begin, typically, by reducing the number of poets whose immediate concern, circa 1914, was, in Williams' words, "the poetic line, the way the image was to lie on the page." Of these, Williams himself, because his verse line remained "open," fared relatively poorly—though never a complete wipe-out like others of whom I'll be speaking later on. Pound managed better but with the stress on the "classicist," fussier side of his early poetics, & Eliot (along with British poets like Yeats) did extremely well. There was also a tendency to include as "modern" a number of conventional or moderately reformist poets like Robinson or Frost—many of whom were more suitable models for the middle-grounders. Among earlier American poets, Dickinson, Poe or Lanier were nearly always possible; Whitman hardly ever.

The idea was, understandably, to lay a reasonable groundwork for the poetry of the inheritors. In the 1920s these included poets like Tate & Ransom (with Hart Crane—praised for his "failure"—somewhere in the wings) or a somewhat younger British poet like Auden, whose metrics & intellectual banter were crucial to the middle-ground of American poetry in the 30s & 40s. (For others, Yvor Winters, who broke from a radical position in the 1920s to a beleaguered traditionalism later on, served a similar role.) In the 30s & 40s poets like

Schwartz & Roethke took up similar terrain, joined by such as Lowell, Wilbur & Jarrell, each of considerable importance at the apex of Schwartz's "revolution in poetic taste" & through its decline since then. At the point of the Hall-Pack-Simpson *Anthology of New American & British Poets* (1957), the "revolution" had nearly come full circle (like tastes in furniture, etc.) to a genuine Victorian revival.

3.
Counter-Poetics

While all of this was going on, a series of avant-garde emergences was throwing the middle-ground strategy into doubt. The new groupings appearing in the mid-50s (Black Mountain, Beats, the New York school, deep image, concrete poetry, chance processes, etc.) re-explored the idea of an avant-garde, with nearly complete indifference to academic strictures. Poetry was transformative, not only of its present & future, but of its past as well. Primitive & archaic, esoteric & subterranean, non-Western & foreign, each had a part to play in a greater "great tradition." Wrote Gary Snyder: "We are witnessing a surfacing (in a specifically 'American' incarnation) of the Great Subculture which goes back as far perhaps as the late Paleolithic."

In that charged atmosphere, the immediate past (but specifically the idea of "poetic revolution") was also undergoing changes. Charles Olson presented his "projective verse" as a synthesis of experiments by "Cummings, Pound, Williams" & pointed to the "objectivists" of the early 1930s as crucial to the process. New magazines like *Black Mountain Review* & *Origin* began to attend to poets like Rexroth & Zukofsky, while Jonathan Williams's Jargon Press was systematically restoring work by Lowenfels, Zukofsky, Patchen, Mina Loy, Bob Brown, etc. Elsewhere James Schuyler, speaking for himself & poets like Frank O'Hara, wrote: "Duchamp's . . . Rrose Selavy has more to do with poetry written by the poets that I know than that Empress of Tapioca, the White Goddess." And Duchamp was also a force behind the chance poetry & music of such as John Cage & Jackson Mac Low—along with Gertrude Stein, whose presence (ignored by the quasi-"Moderns") was of pivotal importance for poets from Robert Duncan to David Antin to Ted Berrigan to, needless to say, the present writer. Or ranging further, Allen Ginsberg left no doubt about his generation's relation to Whitman & Blake, as well as continuities from despised free-verse traditions, rhythm & blues, & the ideological & behavioral implications of Surrealism as mediated by American magazines like *Transition, View* & *VVV*. Other ties to the European & Latin-American avant-gardes were at the heart of "deep image" theory & practice, while concrete poetry was a development from European poets like Apollinaire & the Dutch De Stijl movement, along with Americans as well known as E. E. Cummings or as submerged as Harry Crosby.

With all that in mind, the progress of American poetry takes on a very different shape—not just a change of names or personnel but a counterpoetics that presents (if I can bring it all together by a great simplification) a fundamentally new view of the relationship between consciousness, language & poetic structure: what is seen, said & made. In the working out of that relationship lies the great strength of modern poetry as I understand it. And because the line of the New Critics, etc., failed to confront it meaningfully, their work (though it remains the "official" account of the period) seems to me a backwash rather than a living center.

The turning point, anyway, is just before & during World War I, & the range of poets whose work applies is considerable, highly individualized, & very difficult to pin down. But from where I am at present, I'll try to outline some of the questions & propositions I find of interest then & now & (crucial to the story of this book) in the time between:

(1) There is a widespread feeling circa 1914 that consciousness (man's awareness of himself in time & space) is changing. This is taken as both a crisis & an opportunity, & presupposes a continuous need to confront & to integrate new experience & information. A common explanation connects this change, alteration or expansion of consciousness with technological change (the basic condition of the *modern* world) or, more specifically, with a revolution in communications & an easing

of cultural & psychic boundaries that together produce an "assault" of alternative ideas & forms. In a world in which "so much happens and anybody at any moment knows everything that is happening," Gertrude Stein sees the artist as the person who "inevitably has to do what is really exciting." And when Pound writes (1915) of a basic poetic process that involves "a rush of experience into the vortex" (i.e., the mind), he is talking about a condition that has become newly critical.

(2) In terms of his immediate experience, the modern poet often shares with his ancient prototype, the shaman, a fundamental concern with the thing seen. He is himself the one who sees & projects his vision to others. The individuality of his vision & the stress he puts on it may vary, & he may speak of in-sight or of objectification: the intensification of ego or its suppression. No poet solves the problem of vision under these changed circumstances, & by our own time, it becomes evident that the function of poetry isn't to impose a single vision or consciousness but to liberate similar processes in others. The point, which will come up again & again in this anthology, is that the concern with "seeing" is at the heart of the enterprise: e.g., Pound's "image" as the "primary pigment of poetry"; Stein's change of the thing seen as the key to composition; Crane's "poetic prophecy" qua "perception"; Oppen's faith that "the virtue of the mind is that emotion which causes to see"; even Duchamp's "shop window proof of the existence of the exterior world," etc.*

(3) When the poet confronts still different kinds of knowing, sees himself with others in *time*, the "rush of experience" opens into history. In American poetry, this concern stands prominent. But where the ideas truly "rush," the process no longer links event to event in good straight lines. In the face of multiple chronologies, many poets turn to synchronicity (the simultaneous existence of all places & times) as a basic organizing principle. As a method, a process of making the poem, this becomes "collage": not history but "the dramatic juxtaposition of disparate materials without commitment to explicit syntactical relations between elements" (D. Antin). It is

* See above, page 13, & throughout the "Dialogue on Oral Poetry."

through synchronicity & collage—not only applied to the past but to local & personal particulars—that the modern poem is open to everything; that it becomes the vehicle for "anything the mind can think."

(4) As the "poetic domain" expands to include the possibility of all human experience, a medium is needed flexible enough to get it said. To project the rush of disparate ideas & images (both a lot & a little), poets turn to every means afforded by language: "all words that exist in use" (Whitman), all levels & styles of language, borrowings from other languages, new words or word distortions (punnings), visual signs, experiments with animal & mediumistic language, even clichés & old poeticisms where the content demands it. Metrics give way to measure—"not the sequence of the metronome" (Pound) but a variable succession of sounds & silences, breath- or mind-directed, a "musical line" derived from the complex movements of actual speech. The written text becomes the poem's notation or, in the formulation of visual & concrete poets, a space in which the eye reads visible shape & meaning at a single glance. Here & there too, one sees the first experiments with performance & a fusion with the other arts—toward "intermedia" & the freedom of a poetry without fixed limits, which may change at any point into something else.

(5) With such means at his disposal, the poet can enter on a career as a prophet & revolutionary, a cultist or a populist by turns. Or he can, in a more profound sense, become the person who keeps raising alternative propositions, eluding the trap of his own visions as he goes.

4.
Chronology

The idea of a poetry that was revolutionary in structure & word was carried by an "advance guard" (several in fact) from early in the century until the new poetic revolution of the 1950s. In turn these first avant-garde poets had received it, qua prophecy, from poets & artists just before them, as well as from a range of older poetries, subterranean traditions that were being uncovered piecemeal & read as alternative views of poetic origins & the "nature of the real." The roots were set, & by 1913 the new shoots were appearing at the surface.

That year, 1913, is the key to the initial groupings in the present book. Three germinal events to be noted—of which only one, "imagism(e)," is still given sufficient attention in the histories of poetry. A playful move by Pound, as British correspondent for *Poetry*, to provide a "movement" (complete with Frenchified name) for his work, H. D.'s & Richard Aldington's, it offered a series of principles ("do's & don't's") as a "classicist" interpretation of the free verse practiced by earlier American followers of Whitman. But almost immediately it split into the "imagism" of Amy Lowell & others (an amalgam of free verse & haiku, etc.) & Pound's own development of "vorticist" theory over the next several years. Typically enough, it's "imagism" that retains a place in the literary histories, while the vorticist proposals, crucial to one aspect of collage in U.S. poetry, are inevitably left to the "Poundians."

The two other "events" of 1913 were the Armory art show in New York & the appearance, prior to the publication the following year of *Tender Buttons*, of some of Gertrude Stein's writings in a special number of Stieglitz's magazine, *Camera Work*. The Armory Show didn't just introduce European art (cubism, futurism, etc.) to America, but, as witnessed by Williams & others, it "brought to a head" the "great surge of interest in the arts generally" that was "seething" in places like New York & Chicago before World War I. In that context Stein's work appeared as a cubist poetry that went beyond French poets like Apollinaire, offering strategies of composition & language that remain at the limits of modern poetry sixty years later.

This interplay of poetry & art has been viewed with suspicion by those for whom poetry exists in a basically literary framework. Yet it was crucial, & many poets besides Williams & Stein have testified to its importance. After the start of World War I, Pound joined the British novelist & cubist painter Wyndham Lewis in preparation of *Blast,* a polemical, futurist-styled magazine that turned "imagism" into vorticism & set much of the groundwork for Pound's own *Cantos.* In America, *Camera Work* & its successor, *291,* provided a place for both artists & poets, publishing work by Stein & Apollinaire, early writings by the painter-poet Marsden Hartley, & Mina Loy's "Aphorisms on Futurism" (1914), which introduced her as another germinal & now astonishingly neglected poet. And in 1915, Marcel Duchamp came to New York, to settle in the U.S. & contribute work as both an artist (or anti-artist) & a poet writing in French, English & a visual/mental language somewhere beyond both.

The Duchamp nexus is also overlooked & crucial. With Picabia, Man Ray & Walter Conrad Arensberg, Duchamp heated up the general American climate & provided a link between the Zurich Dadaists of 1917 & the American version that preceded them. The local Dada work appeared in several magazines edited by Duchamp & Arensberg, & shared space in *Rogue* & Alfred Kreymborg's *Others.* While nohow as homogeneous as a short summary might make it sound, the "movement" (when supplemented by the wider context provided by Kreymborg & the *Others* group) included poets like Bob Brown, Mina Loy, Else von Freytag-Loringhoven, Maxwell Bodenheim, & Marsden Hartley, along with Williams, who was a link in turn to the Pound-Eliot nexus developing in Britain. And in Chicago, *The Little Review* (edited by Margaret Anderson & Jane Heap) provided similar juxtapositions of the new poetry, by following a year of Pound's guest editorship that focused on himself, Eliot, Joyce, Yeats, & Lewis, with a heavy concentration on poets like Freytag-Loringhoven, Loy, & Stein, installments of Joyce's *Ulysses,* & an attempt through the early 20s to keep the European avant-garde at the center of American attentions.

During that first post-war decade, many of the early poets remained central to the new developments—or, like Williams, increased their range & influence. Still others like Stevens & Cummings took independent positions that covered additional areas of structure & vision. And the first "disappearances" began: Duchamp's exaggerated withdrawal from art (while his writings as Rrose Selavy went on in French), Else von Freytag-Loringhoven's return to Europe & a tragic death, & the increasing silence of Mina Loy after portions of her long poem, "Anglo-Mongrels & the Rose," appeared in installments in *The Little Review* & Robert McAlmon's *Contact.*

The Surrealists had by then begun to move in European poetry & art, & the influence though not the institution spread to America as well. Outside France, the political & social sides of the movement weakened considerably, while its psychic aspects (the incorporation of dream into everyday life, etc.) had a variety of effects, from thickening the avant-garde plot & helping to trigger the later psychedelic revolution, to becoming a kind of fashionable window dressing, devoid of its initial freedom & terror. Nor was it only the Surrealists who carried the message. Eliot's *Waste Land,* when it appeared, wasn't the simple "catastrophe" described by Williams, but coincided with the haunted world of Surrealism, where:

. . . bats with baby faces in the violet light
Whistled, and beat their wings
And crawled head downward down a blackened wall
And upside down in air were towers. . .

And it was also the first American poem on deliberate collage principles to surface & exert an influence on modern poetry throughout the world.

The "crisis in consciousness" (Mina Loy, 1914) had become overt. Questions of "vision" & the "thing seen" (or dreamed, etc.) began to dominate avant-garde poetry, often to the neglect of parallel questions of "structure" & "language." Hart Crane, for example, used a form of collage construction as a means for "prophecy" but drew back from any serious reconstitution of the verse line, opting finally for a return to the older "poetic" language. Thus he stands between poets like Allen Tate on his "right" & Harry Crosby on his "left," with both of whom he had significant contacts. Crosby, whose Black Sun Press in Paris first published Crane's *The Bridge,* was a poet whose mythic obsessions (sun gods & goddesses, etc.) surfaced in a variety of new forms: prose poems, long verse incantations, & early concrete & found poetry. He shares a position, strongly influenced by the Surrealists & early vision/structure experimenters like Blake, Rimbaud & Lautreamont, with Eugene Jolas & even younger poets like Charles Henri Ford & Parker Tyler. Jolas' *Transition* (slogan: "the revolution of the word") brought together Surrealist "dream-time" with extensions, by such as Joyce, Stein, & the nearly forgotten Abraham Lincoln Gillespie, of what Pound called *logopoeia* ("a dance of the intelligence among words . . .")—though obviously beyond Pound's tolerance for same.

Elsewhere many poets, responding to the intensifying politics of the 20s & 30s, found the open verse line, related use of speech rhythms, & incorporative techniques like collage, viable instruments for a new public & political poetry. If the anthologies & histories give the impression that modern American poetry was dominated by poets far to the right of their European counterparts, it's partly because they represent the work of the 20s & 30s by poets who were conservative in most aspects of their lives. Social poetry (so-called) has been too easily disdained by the middle-grounders, although many of the poets sometimes identified with it (Patchen, Lowenfels, Fearing, Rukeyser, etc.) were also important in the development of other avant-garde concerns & stances that would serve as models for poets & counter-culturists after World War II.

It's a curious fact too that the younger American poets who developed the structural side of the equation & explored vision as a process of eye & mind ("Objectivism") were all at the same time involved in left-wing politics. Zukofsky, Oppen, Reznikoff, & Rakosi are the "Objectivists" who have re-emerged over the last twenty years as the precursors of some of the dominant post-World War II strategies. Allying themselves with Pound & Williams (but note the differences in political stance) they developed unique extensions of imagist & vorticist poetics—toward what Zukofsky called "the direction of historic & contemporary particulars." Zukofsky, who acted as their theoretician & compiler (*An "Objectivists"*

Anthology, 1932), was one of the most far-reaching innovators on the whole American side of the modernist enterprise, yet neglected with the others until his rediscovery, circa 1950, by the Black Mountain poets. His career in that way is a little like Kenneth Rexroth's, some of whose long poems from the 20s he published in his anthology & the "Objectivists" issue of *Poetry* (1931). While Rexroth was probably too independent to accept the "objectivists" association, he had developed an "objective" collage technique of his own, which he identified with "literary cubism" as a "restructuring of experience . . . purposive, not dreamlike . . . an uncanniness fundamentally different in kind from the most haunted utterances of the Surrealist or Symbolist unconscious."

By World War II, the avant-garde publishing network (much of it in Europe) had been badly disrupted, & in the hiatus that followed, the universities & a sprinkling of literary "reviews" stood out as the purveyors of a highly attentuated modernism, mediated by the Nashville Critics, etc., whose way was made easier by a growing avant-garde inability to reconcile the demands of structure & vision. Some poets like Oppen & Lowenfels had stopped writing; others like Zukofsky had withdrawn; & still others had made a resigned truce with the high-riding new traditionalists. But the presence in New York of Breton & other Surrealist exiles made some difference even then, & a number of magazines & little presses (*View, VVV,* Bern Porter's publications in California) offered a transitional alliance of poets & artists, basically surrealist in outlook. So the enterprise continued, marked by new appearances, whose significance would only become clear in the following decade: Robert Duncan as co-editor of *The Experimental Review;* Philip Lamantia as a 15-year-old poet discovered by Breton; Charles Olson, right after the war, as the last American poet published by the Crosbys' Black Sun Press; & others, like Mac Low & Cage, not out in public yet as poets. The lines of transmission were tangled but they were clearly there, & a new generation was already born & waiting to receive & extend them. . . .

PRE-FACE V:
ORIGINS (1975)

[*An introduction to the collection of "creation texts from the ancient Mediterranean," co-edited & translated by Charles Doria & Harris Lenowitz.*]

What is presented here, these cosmogonies retold, is the paramount interest, & the work of the two who present it is an interest almost equal; & all of it is crucial to the development, the unfolding, changing recovery of cultures and civilizations, that is now to enter its latest phase. Nearly two hundred years have elapsed since that possibility began emerging with the code breakers, the scholars out of Romanticism & driven by the same impulse as its poets, who drew meaning from hieroglyph & wedge, brought the old languages to light—& with those others (searchers & seers again) who needed, demanded, the subterranean & heretical texts that dominant religions & power elites had suppressed for centuries. A historical reconstruction to start with, it was at once more than that: a present concern turned backward, to see the past anew & to allow it to enter into the process of our own self-transformation. "We live," Charles Olson wrote nearly two decades ago, "in an age in which inherited literature is being hit from two sides, from contemporary writers who are laying bases of new discourse at the same time that . . . scholars . . . are making available pre-Homeric & pre-Mosaic texts which are themselves eye-openers."

The gathering that follows has over sixty such eye-openers. Many have never been translated directly into English, almost none (save for an item like the Hittite *Ulikummi,* which Olson himself once handled) into the kind of language that Doria & Lenowitz provide for us here. The change—in the language & structure, the idea in short of what a poem is— isn't peripheral but central, symptomatic of a complex of openings in the aftermath of the two-pronged attack alluded to above. In the paradigm that many of us have come to follow as poets, it's the language that causes us to see, that here can make poetry again from the lifeless things these words were in the first stages of their disinterment. So, as the discourse comes to life now in what these two are doing, the past begins to speak through them—at least an image of the meaning & range of the past that no other means could give.

It seems so right here, so alive, that one wonders why it took this long in coming: why, for example, no collection before this had gone back to, translated the available materials around a single topic to provide a "unified field" view of the subject. What happened historically can explain the present situation. Before 1800 our main sources of information for the religion & mythology, the poetry in short, of the ancient world, were classical Greek & Hebrew: Homer & the Bible. Each language had its established works, its canon, & each canon was sufficient to define a classical & sacred tradition: a field for truth & imagination which set the boundaries of reality for man & God. And if our present "curriculum"—whatever classical curriculum remains in schools or on the great books lists—may seem not to have changed much, our actual knowledge has grown through those recoveries that have unearthed & deciphered a score of ancient languages or have revealed alternative traditions in languages already known. Through the nineteenth century & up to the present, specialists have been able to regain & reconstruct much of the poetry of the ancient Near East. And this has led in turn to the publication of poems like the *Epic of Gilgamesh,* the Egyptian *Book of the Dead,* the *Ulikummi,* & the *Enuma Elish* (Babylonian creation cycle): most in translations that have barely gotten under the skin of the originals or have, as strategy for recovery of the poem, put it into the language of our conventional & orthodox past.

But for all of that poetic conservatism (& the other conservatisms it has often masked), the historical, mythical, & ethnic realities have continued changing. No longer need one think of Western religion & philosophy as split between two essentially separate traditions: Hellenic & Hebraic. Greek &

Hebrew poetry can be read in a new light—shed by literatures older & at least as complex, which paralleled, if not actually influenced, them & which pointed to the existence of an even larger Euro-Mediterranean culture complex. In addition, alternative Greek & Hebrew texts, often outside the established traditions, have continued to come to light: the sacred writings of pagans & of gnostic heretics that make an even stronger case for a redefined network of cultural continuities.

Clearly all of this has involved more than pure, disinterested research, as the orthodox defenders, the puritan censors, realized from the start, along with those adventuresome scholars & poets who recognized that the history & roots of our civilization needed to be re-examined & revised in light of the new knowledge. From the latter point of view it was obvious, for example, that such accepted literary forms as epic, drama, history, & so on didn't begin with the Greeks & Hebrews. Not only that, but these categories (the boundaries of which were clearly overlapping) were themselves preceded by an earlier one, the "theogony," & viewed in the light of new concerns with language & function, could be supplemented by forms more in line with contemporary practice: definition, naming, mantra, myth & dream, event & ritual, & so on.

Yet the resistance to popularizing this knowledge was initially widespread: based on prejudices so deeply engrained in the culture that they could hardly be acknowledged until fairly recently. Feelings about Aryan superiority, say, kept many from accepting even the possibility that Homer & Hesiod could have come under Semitic influence—much less the fact. The Greeks had to be narrowly Indo-European or their contribution to Western civilization couldn't be taken seriously. To undermine that uniqueness—blurring long-established distinctions between Jew & Greek—was to strike at the supposed strengths & virtues of Aryan Europe & America.

Religious interests had a parallel stake in maintaining the separateness of the Jewish experience from that of the pre-Christian "nations." And insofar as the scholars were "orthodox" & the texts "pagan" & "heretical," their ideological prejudices hindered translations & studies free from doctrinal

& dogmatic preconceptions. In this context it was difficult to empathize with the older texts, to see one's work as part of the transmission of religious & poetic forms that one viewed as superseded or inimical to the "authentic" Christian &/or Jewish revelation. So, for example, many of the "matriarchal" features in pre-Classical & pre-Hebraic literature were treated at best as relics or mere data, even more so when they turned up in Christian works, say, whose initial republication was hedged around by cautionary explications. The puritanism of many of the early editors (or their response to the puritanism around them) also prevented the full & open handling of the erotic & sexual elements in the newly discovered materials—as it had also in long-recognized traditional texts.

Even where much sympathy was present—in Kramer's *Mythologies of the Ancient World,* say, or Pritchard's *Ancient Near Eastern Texts Relating to the Old Testament*—the results, the proof of the work in the poetry, were often ineffective. Almost unconsciously the translators held back, played down their own efforts, as if they were involved in an antiquarian discipline without much interest for the general reader. The language of the translations, the verse itself where verse was aimed at, was too hesitant: the translator as unwilling poet unable to make the leap that would recover the ancient vision & assist the search for primary modes of poetic & religious experience. Or when scholars like Victor Bérard pointed out a community of culture & folkways between Europe & the Near East, their work was dismissed or neglected —this in spite of the use to which Pound & Joyce, say, put Bérard's postulate of a Semitic Odysseus.

But it was among the latter—"contemporary writers laying the bases of new discourse"—that the scope & intensity of the materials were first revealed. Poets specifically & commentators with a less specialized, more universal view of the matter (Olson, Duncan, Snyder, Kelly, Schwerner in his reinvented *Tablets,* Graves & Eliade & Campbell) offered visions of ancient Europes, Asias, Africas, whole worlds united by what Olson called the "pleistocene" or Snyder "the Great Subculture (of illuminati) which goes back as far perhaps as the late Paleolithic." Yet mostly they worked off scattered, bowdlerized translations, taken, *faute de mieux,* at face. The poet's mind supplied the missing force, the linkage: not directly in translation but at a third or fourth remove. The results came first as poems, & that sequence of events may in the long run have set the ground for a new order of translation deriving from the *nous poetikos* as a source of energy & form.

The present gathering is a new phase in the process. For the first time the energy enters directly in translation, not as a fluke, an isolated instance, but a full compendium from languages like Hebrew, Greek, Latin, Hittite, Akkadian (Babylonian), Ugaritic (Phoenician, Canaanite), & Egyptian. With their time & place the ancient Mediterranean before the triumph of Christianity & Islam, the editors have concentrated on a central, primal idea, *cosmogony,* the narrative of cosmic origins, & have gathered an unprecedented range of texts around it. These materials aren't taken as philosophy or theology *per se* but as *poesis:* the making or shaping of reality through speech—myth emerging naturally by way of mouth to ear.* The narrative here is constantly in the process of defining itself: not the recollection of an ur-text but mind as witness to its own creations.

To bring across this sense of myth as process & conflict, Lenowitz & Doria, working as both poets & scholars, make use of all those "advances in translation technique, notation, & sympathy" developed over the last few decades, from the methods of projective verse to those of etymological translation or of that attention to the recovery of the oral dimension of the poem that the present writer & others have, wisely or not, spoken of elsewhere as "total translation." [See above, page 76.] The picture that emerges is one of richness, fecundity at every turning, from the first image of poem on page to the constantly new insights into the possibilities of "origin." To the latter end the editors offer a wealth of texts never before translated into English (or translated only in relatively inaccessible scholarly publications), along with more familiar

---

* For later comments on *poesis,* see below, page 120.

texts reinterpreted: Lenowitz's polyvalent Genesis, for example, or Doria's reconstitution of Empedocles as "magician, weatherman, & raiser of the dead." Hesiod & Homer, Ovid & Vergil, the Yahvist & the psalmists are here seen freshly, surprisingly, as part of a world with rhapsodic, light-struck Orphists, with Pythagoreans mapping out their worlds through numbers, with early kabbalists exploring alphabetic powers. The work moves from the simplicity of Euripides' ". . . not my story/but one my mother tells" to surreal assemblages of hidden forms & names: the hermaphroditic Elohim & snake/ cunt woman of Justin's *Baruch* (leading by stages to the primal god, Priapus) or that recurrent female body-of-the world qua dragon whom even Yahveh knew. And this allows that "clash of symbols" which, those like Paul Ricoeur tell us, both is natural to mind & forms its one sure hedge against idolatry.

The editors comment little, but go about the more fundamental process of constructing a world of possibilities: not a single sacred work of genesis but a space in which all works can come to light. Here the "imaginations of men's thoughts" are no longer the evil that God saw continually but the recurring, strangely shifting *gnosis,* reflective of a wider community than heretofore known, with its roots into that older universal shamanism the West would later try to live without. To get this in the open, Doria & Lenowitz let the words (both of their sources & their own) enter again into that process of becoming—as if to begin anew the old work of *formation.*

And that is so much the achievement of this true source book: its great unifying image for poet & general reader alike. It is a presence still, a power & possibility that outlives the terror of its source. In that way the work is never merely literary, never ancient history, but contemporary with all our other works: the very thing we seek in our pursuit of those particulars, even contraries, that open on the universal vision.

PRE-FACE V:
A BIG JEWISH BOOK (1978)

1.

There was a dream that came before the book, & I might as well tell it. I was in a house identified by someone as THE HOUSE OF JEWS, where there were many friends gathered, maybe everyone I knew. Whether they were Jews or not was unimportant: I was & because I was I had to lead them through it. But we were halted at the entrance to a room, not a room really, more like a great black hole in space. I was frightened & exhilarated, both at once, but like the others I held back before that darkness. The question came to be the room's name, as if to give the room a *name* would open it. I knew that, & I strained my eyes & body to get near the room, where I could feel, as though a voice was whispering to me, creation going on inside it. And I said that it was called CREATION.

I now recognize that dream as central to my life, an event & mystery that has dogged me from the start. I know that there are other mysteries—for others, or for myself at other times, more central—& that they may or may not be the same. But CREATION—*poesis* writ large—appeared to me first in that house, for I was aware then, & even more so now, that there are Jewish mysteries that one confronts in a place no less dangerous or real than that abyss of the Aztecs:

> . . . a difficult, a dangerous place, a deathly place. It is dark, it is light. *

& with a sense too that this space must be bridged, this door opened as well—the door made just for you, says the guardian in Kafka's story. Yet Kafka, like so many of us, poses the other question also: "What have I in common with Jews? I have hardly anything in common with myself. . . ."

* See below, page 149.

For myself it had suddenly seemed possible—this was in 1966 or '67 & I was finishing *Technicians of the Sacred*—to break into that other place, "my own . . . a world of Jewish mystics, thieves, & madmen." From that point on, it opened up in stages. Images, once general & without particular names, now had identified themselves. I let my mind—& the words of others, for I had learned as well to collage & assemble—work out its vision of "fantastic life," as Robert Duncan had called it for all poetry: an image in this instance of some supreme Yiddish surrealist vaudeville I could set in motion. With those poems *(Poland/1931)* I made a small entry, American & Eastern European; yet something had dropped away, so that it was now possible to be "in common with myself," to experience the mystery of naming, like the thrill & terror of my Jewish dream.

Still the event wasn't "mine" but part of a process of recovery in our time, of the "long forbidden voices" invoked by Whitman over a century ago, the "symposium of the whole" set forth in Robert Duncan's "rites," now pulling all our impulses together:

> . . . The female, the proletariat, the foreign; the animal and vegetative; the unconscious and the unknown; the criminal and failure—all that has been outcast and vagabond must return to be admitted in the creation of what we consider we are. (R.D.)

And the Jew too among the "old excluded orders," not in the name of "the incomparable nation or race, the incomparable Jehovah in the shape of a man, the incomparable Book of Vision," but come into "the dream of everyone, everywhere." A primal people, then, as instance of those cultures of the old worlds, built through centuries of preparation, not to be repeated, whose universality arises, like all others, from its own locations, its particulars in space & time.

The work of many, poets & others, has gone into that process, both inventing & re-inventing—the Jewish side of which turns up for us in contemporaries like Paul Celan, Jack Hirschman, Edmond Jabès, David Meltzer, Rochelle Owens,

Nathaniel Tarn, as well as others, friends or enemies, who struggle with that Jewish daemon, force us to renew, to make again, the statement of the great refusal. Jewish, human at the core.

2.

The work, as set out here, includes both terms, the Jewish & the human. In that second, larger frame—of which the first is, for myself, a central & sufficient instance—the matters that touch on the "recovery" are, first, the idea of *poesis* as a primary human process; second, the primacy of the "oral tradition" in *poesis;* third, the re-invigoration of the bond between ourselves & other living beings; fourth, the exploration of a common ground for "history" & "dream-time" (myth); & fifth, the "re-invention of human liberty" (S. Diamond) in the shadow of the total state.* These are the keys to any "modernism" still worth its salt. And they are the keys also to the oldest poetry we know: that of the shaman-poets, "technicians of the sacred," whose visionary use of song & speech had its roots, by every mark we've learned to read, back into the Old Stone Age. And, it was just this poetry, this language-of-vision in a culture that was communalistic, anarchic & egalitarian, that the newer city-states tried to destroy, no less in Judaea—where the cry was "thou shalt not suffer a shaman to live"—than in other civilizations throughout the world.

* By *poesis* I mean a language process, a "sacred action" (A. Breton) by which a human being creates & recreates the circumstances & experiences of a real world, even where such circumstances may be rationalized otherwise as "contrary to fact." It is what happens, e.g., when the Cuna Indian shaman of Panama "enters"—as a landscape "peopled with fantastic monsters & dangerous animals"—the uterus of a woman suffering in childbirth & relates his journey & his struggle, providing her, as Lévi-Strauss tells it, "with a language by means of which unexpressed or otherwise inexpressible psychic states can be immediately expressed." This "power of the word," while often denied or reduced to posturings or lies in the "higher" civilizations, has continued as a tradition among poets & others who feel a need to "express the inexpressible"—a belief in what William Blake called "double vision" or, in Lévi-Strauss's paraphrasing of Rimbaud, that " 'metaphor' can change the world."

The poet, if he knows his sources in the "sacred actions" of the early shamans, suffers anew the pain of their destruction. In place of a primitive "order of custom," he confronts the "stony law" & "cruel commands" Blake wrote of—"the hand of jealousy among the flaming hair." Still he confirms, with Gary Snyder, the presence of a "Great Subculture (of illuminati)" within the higher civilizations [see above, page 115], an alternative tradition or series of traditions hidden sometimes at the heart of the established order, & a poetry grudgingly granted its "license" to resist. No minor channel, it is the poetic *mainstream* that he finds here: magic, myth, & dream; earth, nature, orgy, love; the female presence the Jewish poets named Shekinah.

In the Jewish instance—as my own "main main"—I can now see, no longer faintly, a tradition of *poesis* that goes from the interdicted shamans (= witches, sorcerers, etc., in the English Bible) to the prophets & apocalyptists (later "seers" who denied their sources in their shaman predecessors) & from there to the merkaba & kabbala mystics, on the right hand, & the gnostic heretics & nihilist messiahs, on the left.* But I don't equate it with mysticism *per se* ("which appears to love a mystery as much outside as it does in," writes Charles Olson), rather prize it in every breakthrough of "poetic mind"—that drive to *make it new* (E. Pound), to pit the old transformative ways of thought against the other, intervening drive toward an authoritative written text &, what confronts us once again, the reduction of particulars to what has become the monoculture. I would expect it, as much as anywhere else, in the secular poets of our own time, even or most particularly those who resemble what Gershom Scholem calls "nihilist mystics," for whom "all authority is rejected in the name of mystical experience or illumination" & who leap, like Rimbaud's seer-poet "into the unknown"—the "cauldron" Gershom Scholem

* This follows roughly the stages (torah, mishna, kabbala, magic & folklore, etc.) by which the "oral tradition" ("torah of the mouth") was narrowed & superseded by the written. But not without resistance; says the *Zohar:* "The Voice should never be separated from the Utterance, & he who separates them becomes dumb &, being bereft of speech, returns to dust." An ongoing concern here.

names it, place of "promiscuity," etc., "in which the freedom of living things is born." Separated from mysticism, *poesis* persists as process, as preparation: it is evolving, contradictory, not fixed or rigid but "with an infinite capacity for taking on new forms." The poet meets the mystic where "their end, their aim"—wrote Moses Porges, 1794—"is liberation from spiritual & political oppression."

Now, all of this I would have stressed in any approach to the development of *poesis* in the "West"—an area I deliberately avoided when I was compiling *Technicians of the Sacred*. Before coming to the idea of "a big Jewish book," I had in fact played with the possibility of a pan-European gathering. But that seemed too diffuse for present purposes, & I thought to speak instead from the Jewish instance, which, through diaspora, would still touch all bases, European & more than European—& from an idea too that the specific & even local circumstances (of which I was certainly a part) provided the most direct line for poetic vision. In its Jewish form, then, I could isolate a series of topics & conflicts, tensions, that were either unique or more developed there than elsewhere, or that were developed with concrete, often "dramatic" particulars that formed a hedge against "abstraction" & mere "objectivity." While most turn up in the texts & commentaries in this book, there are a few I would stress as those that hold me to the Jewish work:

- a sense of exile both as cosmic principle (exile of God from God, etc.) & as the Jewish fate, experienced as the alienation of group & individual, so that the myth (gnostic or orthodox) is never only symbol but history, experience, as well;

- from which there comes a distancing from nature & from God (infinite, ineffable), but countered in turn by a *poesis* older than the Jews, still based on namings, on an imaging of faces, bodies, powers, a working out of possibilities (but, principally, the female side of God—Shekinah—as Herself in exile) evaded by orthodoxy, now returning to astound us;

• or, projected into language, a sense (in Jabès's phrase) of being "exiled in the word"—a conflict, as I read it, with a text, a web of letters, which can capture, captivate, can force the mind toward abstract pattern or, conversely, toward the framing, raising, of an endless, truly Jewish "book of questions";

• &, finally, the Jews identified as mental rebels, who refuse consensus, thus become—even when bound to their own Law, or in the face of "holocaust," etc.—the model for the Great Refusal to the lie of Church & State.

And it's from such a model—however obscured by intervening degradations from *poesis,* impulse to conform, etc.—that I would understand Marina Tsvetayeva's dictum that "all poets are Jews."

3.

If this keeps me attached to the "history of the Jews" & identified with it, I realize too that the terms in which I present it often go beyond what has seemed reasonable to those living within it. Like other peoples with a long history of life under the gun, Jews have tended in their self-presentation (whether to themselves or others) to create an image that would show them in the "best light" & with the least possibility of antagonizing their oppressors. By doing so we have often denied ourselves the assertion of a full & multi-sided humanity, choosing to present an image that was gentle, passive, sensitive, & virtuous, & that in its avoidance of complication tended to deny negative emotions or experiences & to avoid claims to ideas & personalities that our antagonists had staked out as their own. This was further assisted by the circumscriptions of Jewish orthodoxy, with its concept of the single immutable vision & text, & with its hostility to innovators & counter-culturists among its own people. For many Jewish poets & artists, working within a Jewish context came to mean the surrender of claims to the sinister & dangerous sides of existence or to participation in the fullest range of historical human experience. In the process many came to confuse the defensive or idealized image with the historical & to forget that the actual history of the Jews was as rich in powers & contradictions as that of the surrounding nations.

Once into this book, it also seemed to me that much that I had taken for granted about the Jewish past—& present— no longer held up. Since such discoveries influenced my further work, even as I made them, I think I should present some of them here—or present them (for economy) along with a series of statements on the sources & boundaries of this book.

As supreme wanderers—even before & after the forced diaspora—the Jews' historical & geographical range has been extraordinary. To map this in "a big Jewish book," I have included works from the ancient Jewish languages—Hebrew & Aramaic—& from those like Yiddish & Ladino developed in the course of exile, as well as from other languages (Greek, Spanish, Arabic, German, English, Persian, French, etc.) used by Jews in Biblical & post-Biblical times. But I have been impressed as well by the continuity of a specifically Hebrew poetry which, far from being stifled in the aftermath of "Bible," has produced a series of new forms & visualizations, the diversity of which is in itself a matter of much wonder.

Alongside this continuity, there are three turning points in the history of Jewish consciousness that I would stress here:

- a shift, early along, from both the older shamanism & the general pattern of ancient Near Eastern religion to the centralized & gradually dominant monotheism of the Priests & Prophets;

- a series of changes around the time of Jesus (but really from a century or two before to a century or two after), in which the Jews—as a *large* & mobile population,* scattered

* Recent estimates for the 1st century B.C. set the Jewish population as high as 8 million, thus 6–9% of the Roman Empire, 20% of the eastern provinces, 33% of Alexandria, etc. (Michael Grant, *The Jews in the Roman World*, page 60, plus relevant sections in Louis Finkelstein, *The Jews: Their History, Culture, & Religion*.) And prior to their later defeat & subjection, the Jews were also heavily into conversion—both full &

throughout the Mediterranean & maintaining an active poetic & religious tradition in both Hebrew & Greek—generated a number of conflicting movements: Christian & gnostic on the one hand, rabbinic, messianic, & kabbalistic on the other;

• with the triumph of Church & Synagogue, the entry of Jewish consciousness into an extraordinary subterranean existence that would erupt later in a series of libertarian movements: within a Jewish frame, the seventeenth- & eighteenth-century Sabbateans & Frankists, twentieth-century Zionists, etc., & outside it the critical role of Jews & ex-Jews in revolutionary politics (Marx, Trotsky, etc.) & avant-garde poetics (Tzara, Kafka, Stein, etc.).

Work for this book has accordingy been drawn from both "sacred" & "secular" sources, with the link between them *my* stress on a poetic/visionary continuum & on the mystical & magical side of the Jewish tradition. And since poetry, in the consensus of my contemporaries, is more concerned with the "free play of the imagination" than with doctrinal certainties *per se,* I've made no attempt to establish an "orthodox" line or to isolate any one strain as purer or more purely Jewish than any others. Instead my assumption has been that poetry, here as elsewhere, is an inherently impure activity of individuals creating reality from all conditions & influences at hand.

Concretely this non-doctrinal approach has called for attention to sources like the following, many not usually found in such a gathering:

• tribal & polytheistic remnants, like the battle of Yahveh & the Sea Serpent, the story of Lilith, the accounts of the Sons of God, even Ugaritic (Canaanite) narratives of Baal & Ashera, etc.;

• non-canonical & "heretical" texts, viewed as a subterranean continuation of the earlier traditions—but principally celestial spirit journeys & power dreams in the work

---

partial—& "almost uniquely among the subjects of Rome . . . were still producing an extensive literature of their own." (M. Grant.)

of merkaba & apocalyptic visionaries; this includes both acknowledged apocrypha (4th Book of Ezra, Book of Enoch, etc.) & more heterodox texts like *Sefer ha-Hekhalot* ("The Book of Palaces"), "The War of the Sons of Light against the Sons of Darkness" from the Dead Sea Scrolls, etc.;

• visionary poetry of early Jewish Christians & Gnostics, including New Testament works like the Book of Revelation, & gnostic ones like the "Round Dance of Jesus" in the Acts of Saint John, or those of messianic figures like Simon Magus, etc.; also anti-Christian writings like the *Toldot Yeshu* counter-gospel;

• kabbala, as the last great oral (thus: secret, whispered) tradition of ancient Judaism, leading from second-century mystics like Simeon bar Yohai & Ishmael ben Elisha to the *Zohar* of Moses de Leon, the discourses & mystic hymns of Isaac Luria, the "abstract" graphics of Abraham Abulafia & Moses Cordovero, the later messianic heresies of Sabbatai Zevi & Jacob Frank, etc.;

• the Jewish magical tradition, in all its manifestations, as a poetry of naming & invocation: ancient texts like the third-century *Sefer ha-Razim* ("The Book of Mysteries"), magical texts in the recognized kabbala & in "spurious" classical & medieval works like the "Book of Moses on the Secret Name," & later oral & folkloristic traditions in Hebrew, Yiddish, Arabic, etc.;

• the poetry of Jewish groups outside the European &/or rabbinical "mainstream": Essenes, Samaritans, Karaites, Falashas, Chinese Jews, etc.;

• previously downgraded figures like the medieval *paytanim:* liturgical poets whose poems (*piyutim*) have remained in prayer books but long been ignored or ridiculed in favor of the more literary & "classical" Hebrew poets of Spain, etc., though many of the latter are shown as well;

• Jewish poems whose forms are derived from other literary traditions, like the Hellenistic *Eisagoge* ("tragedy of Moses") by the tragic poet Ezekielos, or medieval Jewish narratives & epics;

• the work of later Jewish poets, even where it develops into an apparently "anti-Jewish" point of view. (Here the proliferation in our time & place of the Jewish side of *poesis* is itself a point worth making—not only as theme [ancestral poetry, etc.] but in the energy of a large number of poets [Stein, Zukofsky, Ginsberg, Mac Low, etc.] who have been central to the "real work of modern man: to uncover the inner structure & actual boundaries of the mind" [G. Snyder].)

While such sources show some of the ways in which I've tried to break new ground, most of the older matter in the book has in fact been drawn from the generally accepted literature (Bible, Mishna, Talmud, Zohar, etc.) & from poets for whom the problem of "identity" probably never arose. But even here my intention was to stress process over the mere re-statement of earlier ideas (the poem not as a " 'fit' but a unification of experience"—William Carlos Williams) & to return to a sense of the original moment, renewing the poetic event by all means of interpretation (translation) at my disposal. Thus, visionary & dream accounts in the prophetic books (Daniel, Ezekiel, etc.) have been retranslated to emphasize the immediate experience, or the very ancient Song of Deborah has been treated as an oral performance piece or re-enactment by a poet-singer who assumes a range of roles & voices. And, as much here as elsewhere, I have tried to show the many sides of Jewish experience, including instances (e.g., the gloating over Sisra's death in "Deborah," etc.) that went against my grain but revealed some part of the reality.

As in *Technicians of the Sacred,* I have also worked by analogy with contemporary forms of poetry & art, to isolate structures not usually included in the conventional anthologies or not thought of as poetry *per se*. The most striking of these are the many types of language happenings that form the "mantric" base of traditional Jewish mysticism & kabbala: "masoretic" visual poems; word-events used in the transformation of older texts &/or in the creation & discovery of the names of God; sound-poems arising from that naming process or in the wordless chanting of religious celebrants, etc. In addition, various ritual forms have been treated, where relevant, in the manner of intermedia events & happenings, & because of the book's range ("from tribal times to *present*") have been presented alongside contemporary artists & poets like Kaprow, Mac Low, the Living Theatre, etc. Such inclusions have re-enforced my sense that both a contemporary critique of "civilization" & a concern with experimental, often non-ikonic forms of language have a particular resonance & an actual history within the Jewish context. . . .

From PRE-FACE TO A SYMPOSIUM
ON ETHNOPOETICS (1975)

[*In April 1975 I helped Michael Benamou organize the First International Symposium on Ethnopoetics at the Center for 20th Century Studies in Milwaukee. Some remarks of mine opened several days of talk & performance but were largely a rehash of what I had been laying down over the previous ten or fifteen years. A few months after the symposium, I was able to complete the considerations begun there & to read, talk & perform my way around the central question of "poetry & performance" as I felt it in my own & in related work. The occasion was the annual meeting of the American Theater Association in Washington, D.C., & what follows is a composition from notes & tapes.*]

There is a Seneca Indian song, a song that is part of a medicine society & ceremony called "shaking the pumpkin" or "the society of the mystic animals" or "the society of shamans," which I have translated elsewhere in a more elaborate form than I will give here. But it is a key, in what it says, to the bewilderment I feel at where my own poetry & the poetry of my generation has taken me—to this place, for example, where I am to be celebrating a poetry of performance in our time tied up in some ways we have yet to define to a poetry of performance in those cultures we may think of as "primitive" or "primary" or "primal." The words of the Seneca song, which I translated with the Seneca singer, Richard Johnny John, go like this (the title is our own addition):

I WAS SURPRISED TO FIND
MYSELF OUT HERE &
ACTING LIKE A CROW

I didn't think I'd
shake the pumpkin
not just here & now
not exactly tonight

I didn't think I'd
rip some meat off
not just here & now
not exactly tonight

Now, I had not shaken the pumpkin before, had not sung
before or sung before to a rattle: I had not done any of these
things & it would have seemed foolish to me then to have done
them. It did seem foolish but at a point I was doing them & it
no longer seemed foolish, seemed necessary if anything I had
said about it before had a meaning. My own origins, from
which I had been running for most of my grown life, should
have told me as well, if I had been able then to give them my
attention, for the living tradition of the Jews is also "oral,"
from the mouth, & even in an age of writing, the word must be
renewed by the processes of "speaking" & of "sounding." [See
below, page 163.] It is by such sounding & voicing (this near
eruption into song) that the attention is brought to focus on
the sources of the poem, the song, the discourse, in the prior
act of composition (making or receiving), which was itself an
act of focusing attention. In creating that attention, that in-
tensity, the Senecas, who are otherwise as removed as we are
from the primitive condition, begin the ceremony by invoking
those "mystic animals" who were the first keepers of the song,
who came once in a vision to a hunter lost & wounded in the
woods, to cure him & leave him with a set of keys by which to
summon them again. The ceremony begins in darkness, then
the rattle sounds, & makes a kind of light, a heat, that moves
around the circle of those joined in the performance.

*(At this point there follows a chanting, with rattle, of
the opening songs to "Shaking the Pumpkin," translated
by myself & Richard Johnny John.)*

Now, what has happened here, at least for me, is not a sep-
arated series of events or actions but a totality that I no longer
want to break into its component parts: to isolate the words,
say, as the poem. For my experience is the experience of
everything that happens to me in that act: the movement of
my arm, the sound (& feel) of pebbles against horn, the way

that breaks across my voice, the tension in my throat, the full release of breath, the emptying that leaves me weak & ready to receive the next song, the song occurring, rising out of memory, becoming voice, becoming sound, becoming physical again, & then returning into silence. And it is also this room, this time & place, these others here with me. The event is different from the event of composition (in this case, to further complicate the matter, involves a second composition-by-translation), but the poem is everything-that-happens: & if it is, then to insist that it is only part of it (the words), is to mistake the event, to miss that total presence.

Before I am anything else, I am a poet & (living in the time I do) a stand-up performer of my own poetry. It is better for me to *do* poetry than to talk *about* it. I do it first & then I sound it: this is doing it a second time, a third a fourth a fifth time, to renew it by the sounding. My performance is this sounding of a poem: it is renewal of the poem, the poem's enlivening. Without this sounding there would be no poem as I have come to do it (though, since I work by writing, there would be notes about the poem as I intended it). This is the return to voice, to song, as the poet Gary Snyder speaks of it; it is one side of the impulse toward the oral, toward a poetry of performance, as is that other side, discourse, that the poet David Antin speaks of. Poetry becomes the sounding—not the script apart, the preparation or notation, but the sounding. Where there is no writing, the sounding truly renews the poem, creates it in each instance, for here there is no poem without performance. Writing, that strange aid to memory, eventually becomes its surrogate, displaces memory itself—the first, great Muse. The poetry *sounding* becomes the poetry *reading*. This is the condition under which most of us work. If others would go more deeply into orality, would bring composition & performance together in a single improvised event, that would also be welcome. But I would like to describe it as it now is for me & why I have sought my model of the poem-as-performance (the poem in action) in the domain of what I came to call the "ethnopoetic."

As a stand-up performer the poet retains a solitary stance. He is in no way the playwright of the old verse dramas, but the central (typically the *only*) figure in a performance in which he *must* play a part. The part he plays is the poet-as-himself, performing in a theater as yet without an actor—or much of anything else besides what the poet brings: words & a voice. The difference between the poet & the actor is somehow crucial: the basis of the poetry performance is in fact hostile to the presence, the manner, of the professional actor. That the poet as performer is otherwise motivated, otherwise related to the poem, is here a shared assumption: an insistence on a lack of separation between the maker & his work, & of a virtual innocence of any means of performance beyond the ones immediately to hand. The poet's delivery may vary, he may read easily or he may falter, he may digress, he may drift at times into a drunken incoherence, he may fulfill or disappoint our expectations of how a poem is spoken. Somehow it is enough that he has risked himself to do as much as he can do: to stand there as a witness to his words, he who alone can sound them. That kind of witnessing is not without its precedents, as in the sounding of the written "law" within the ancient Jewish Temple, where the reader (sounder) was the witness to the meaning of a text devoid of vowels. It is one arrangement (there are others) that maintains the oral basis of a poetry, its openness, once we have entered on an age of writing. In the poetry of our own time, with its use of an approximate & highly individualized notation, the measure of a poem (& much of its meaning) is likewise only clear when it is being sounded: in this case sounded by its maker. The poet when he sounds his poem is witness to the way it goes, the way it came to happen in the first place. He is in fact the witness to a (prior) vision, to an image-of-the-world expressed through word & sound. The failure to communicate is a failure to communicate his credibility: his own relation to those words, that vision. The actor may attempt to take his place (& in certain kinds of theater today the actors have become the makers & the sounders of their own words), but as a witness to the *poet's* words the actor's credibility has yet to be established.

●

There is a widespread idea that the poets of our time, the artists in general, have abandoned the possibility of relating to poets of other times as models: that we live without a vision of ourselves as historical beings but are locked into an eternal present, not so much an opportunity as a trap. I have never seen our condition in those terms—have rather seen us as freeing ourselves, on the basis of conditions in the world itself, to a wider, more generous view of the past, of the historical totality of human experience, than has ever been possible. This process has been going on at least from the time of the Romantics, & it has produced a number of new images, new models or visions, of the past, from which we now can draw. (Like any historical search, it functions to heighten our awareness of the present & the future.)

Increasingly, the model, the prototype, of the poet has become the "shaman": the solitary, inspired religious functionary of the late paleolithic. [See below, page 134.] Partly this has been because of our own involvement with the kind of solitary, stand-up performance that I was just describing. But there is also a second side to it: the visionary & ecstatic, & a third perhaps: the communal. I will not concentrate on the last two (although they are in some ways the real heart of the matter) but will try to focus on the shaman's (proto-poet's) way of going/speaking/singing: his performance. In a deeper, if often more confused sense, what is involved here is the search for a primal ground: a desire to bypass a civilization that has become problematic & to return, briefly, often by proxy, to the origins of our humanity. Going back in time we continue to find diversity & yet, maybe because we're looking at it from the wrong end, the picture emerges of an intertribal, universal culture (& behind it a poetics) that has a number of discernible, definable features. The most direct inheritors of this culture—up to their virtual disappearance in our time—are those hunting & gathering peoples, remnants of whom now exist as an endangered & ultimately doomed "fourth world." Far from being mere "wild men," mere fantasizing children, they had a world-view marked (Paul Radin tells us) by a strong sense of realism ("reality at white heat") or, according to Stanley Diamond, "(by) modes of thinking (that) are substantially concrete, existential & nominalistic, within a personalistic context" & supremely able to "sustain contradictions."

Here the dominant religious functionary is the shaman: he is the one who sees/the one who sings/the one who heals. He is not yet the bard, the tribal historian. He is not necessarily the speaker. He is typically withdrawn: experiences long periods of silence, other periods of exaltation. He may inherit his words, his songs, from others or he may come on them directly in a vision or a trance. He may be a prolific song-maker or he may be constantly renewing a small, fixed body of song. He may have helpers, but typically he works alone. He may improvise within the actual performance of his rites, but more often he will sound, will activate, the words or song delivered at another time & place.

So, among us the poet has come to play a performance role that resembles that of the shaman. (This is more than coincidence because there is an underlying ideology: communal, ecological, even historical: an identification with late paleolithic ideology & social organization, seen as surviving in the "great subcultures" within the later city-states, civilization, etc.) The poet like the shaman typically withdraws to solitude to find his poem or vision, then returns to sound it, give it life. He performs alone (or very occasionally with assistance, as in the work of Jackson Mac Low, say), because his presence is considered crucial & no other specialist has arisen to *act* in his place. He is also like the shaman in being at once an outsider, yet a person needed for the validation of a certain kind of experience important to the group. And even in societies otherwise hostile or indifferent to poetry as "literature," he may be allowed a range of deviant, even antisocial behavior that many of his fellow-citizens do not enjoy. Again like the shaman, he will not only be allowed to act mad in public, but he will often be expected to do so. The act of the shaman—& his poetry—is like a public act of madness. It is like what the Senecas, in their great dream ceremony now obsolete, called "turning the mind upside down." It shows itself as a release of alternative possibilities. "What do they want?" the poet wonders of those who watch him in his role of innocent, sometimes reluctant performer. But what? To know that madness is possible & that the contradictions can be sustained. From the first shaman—that solitary person—it flows out to whole companies of shamans, to whole societies of human beings: it heals the sickness of the body but more than that: the sickness of the soul. It is a "mode of thinking" & of acting that is "substantially concrete, existential & nominalistic, within a personalistic context" & "supremely able to sustain contradictions." It is the primal exercise of human freedom against/& for the tribe.

●

Now, as many questions are left as are answered. Does the poem really heal? Or what kind of poem or song, or discourse, does heal—or sustain contradictions—or turn the mind upside down? What is the basis for seeing in cultures & poetries so far removed from us the kind of conjunctions I have so far assumed? And if the move from the "oral" to the "literal" was tied up, as I believe it was, with the need of an emergent class of rulers for a more rigorous arrangement of society, why should we now expect a movement in the opposite direction? It is as yet hard to say, for our whole poetics (not just our *ethno*poetics) is, like our life in general, up for grabs. What do we say about the function of our poetry, the thing we do? That it explores. That it initiates thought or action. That it proposes its own displacement. That it allows vulnerability & conflict. That it remains, like the best science, constantly open to change: to a continual change in our idea of what a poem is or may be. What language is. What experience is. What reality is. That for many of us it has become a fundamental process for the play & interchange of possibilities.

And it has come out of a conflict—more or less deeply felt—with inherited forms of poetry, literature, language, discourse: not in every instance but where these are recognized as repressive structures, forms of categorical thinking that act against that other free play of possibilities just alluded to. Against these inherited forms, the conventional literature that no longer fed us, we have both searched for & invented other forms. Some of us have doggedly gone from there to a reviewing of the entire poetic past (of any poetry for that matter outside the immediate neighborhood) from the point of view of the present. Here there are two processes involved—not mutually exclusive. On the one hand the contemporary forms (the new means that we invent) make older forms visible: & on the other hand the forms that we uncover elsewhere help us in the reshaping, the resharpening, of our own tools. The past, come alive, is in motion with us. It is no longer somewhere else but, like the future, *here*—which is the only way it can be, toward a poetry of changes.

Ethnopoetics: A First International Symposium, edited by Michel Benamou & Jerome Rothenberg, *Alcheringa,* new series, Volume 2, Number 2, 1976.

3 / Poetics

The issue, then, has always been language—language & reality, nothing else.

ON ANTHOLOGIES (1978)

The exciting thing about all this is that as it is new it is old and as it is old it is new, but now really we have come to be in our way which is an entirely different way.

—GERTRUDE STEIN, *Narration*

It seems to me that I've been making anthologies for as long as I've been making poems *per se*. I used to do them in my head because no compendium, no gathering was available to help me map the territory that was opening up to us. As a kid I inherited a large desk with a sheet of glass on top, beneath which I would slip in pages of poems—my own & others'—& pictures, etc. that I had been coming across in the stuff I was reading. I used to arrange them to form "shows" of works that seemed, by juxtaposition, to inform each other. I also typed up poems from different places & times & kept them in a series of folders marked *anthology*. That was from high school days & stopped sometime in college, when I started to *buy* books & be deceived by other people's arrangements.

When I reawakened in the later 1950s I discovered Blake saying: "I must either create my own 'system' or be trapped in another's"—for which you might substitute the word "anthology." (The danger of being trapped in your own system as well is more subtle but nohow out of the picture.) I got quickly into doing my own press (Hawk's Well) & magazine (*Poems from the Floating World*). But the magazine was really an anthology & I subtitled it, in my mind at least, "an ongoing anthology of the deep image." In it I brought together contemporary work with work from elsewhere that I felt was along the same track. The idea was that we weren't just doing something new (which we were) but were getting back in our own terms to fundamental ways of seeing & languaging from which we (the larger "we" of the Western enterprise) had long been cut off.

I otherwise dislike anthologies—the ones, I mean, that perpetuate the orders of a limited past & by so doing hold back the real work of the present. On the whole I feel better about the kind of anthology that presents a new move in poetry, like a well-conceived magazine or like a group show in the visual arts. But, except for the contemporary side of *America a Prophecy,* I haven't felt myself pulled in that direction either but remain distrustful of the rigidities & career tactics implicit in the form. My own concern has been with interpretations of past & present—the present foremost but not sufficient in itself. In other words, I've looked for a way of measuring our works & selves against the possibilities of a poetics that's big enough to account for human creativity, human language-making over the broadest span available. I have an idea of history—or a feel for it—that guides me & that changes in the process of pulling it together.

David Antin describes me (both in the anthologies & in poems like *Poland/1931*) as "walking backwards . . . moving away from the things that he's leaving . . . but keeping his eyes on them while backing toward the new terrain, which I suppose he only sees directly when it joins the rest behind him." The perspective, which seems true enough to my experience (if you add a little forward twisting of the head from time to time), led me (with hints from predecessors like Tzara & others) to the discovery of lines between past & present, lines overlooked before that transmitted a crypto-tradition (or series of such) throughout the world. The lines led from poem to poem like strings of light—from past to present or, when I turned my head, from present to past. What I saw as poetry was conditioned by what we make as poetry today. The question invariably comes up: why are those sounds in the Navajo chant taken as a "poem"? And the answer: because Hugo Ball or Kurt Schwitters (or you name them) opened that domain for us. But when they did they also pointed to a possible human continuity that had been broken or at the least obscured: a non-semantic form of utterance to which they were now calling our attention. I have, in taking a look for myself, only continued the process, maybe made some of it more overt.

For this, "anthology" seemed like a terrific instrument, as a means for exploring & keeping before us the dimensions of our humanness—even where our explorations lead us to a language seemingly devoid of meanings. I was drawn first to a search for instances ("primitive" & "archaic") of what was, what seemed—if anything—an overly meaning-full area of mind: the world of "images," of what James Hillman more recently speaks of as the "royal road of soul-making" (Keats's term), or image-making, where "to 'be in soul' is to experience the fantasy in all realities & the basic reality of fantasy." I knew it would be there & I sighted it: the multiple ways it shows up under the turns & twists of the particular cultures that attend to it.

Yet once I was into *Technicians of the Sacred*, the discoveries expanded in the process of searching them out. In particular I began to assemble—under section titles like "A Book of Extensions" & "A Book of Events"—works that were different from but strangely like our own experiments with language, structure & performance. In 1964 I had started a group of my own pared-down quasi-minimal pieces called "Sightings" . . . that didn't need more than a word or two to be operative:

Cages (i)
Wires.

Cages (ii)
Pretending.

Cages (iii)
Moon.

Cages (iv)
Summer.

Cages (v)
Summermoon.

Cages (vi)
Summerflies.

Cages (vii)
Cages.

And at the same time I could spot a similar process in Aboriginal (Australian) song-making [see below, pages 205–7]:

Fire	Fire
Flame	Ashes

●

Urination
Testes
Urination

●

Loincloth
(red)
Loincloth
(white)
Loincloth
(black)

●

"penis"	incisure	incisure
penis	penis	semen

Or, watching Hannah Weiner's flag-code poems, say, my attention was turned simultaneously to African drum language or Plains Indian hand-language poems or Pomo Indian flag & dream language, etc. Dada & Futurist "sound poems" pointed to American Indian ones (Tzara, I later found, had made the point explicitly & fully in relation to African & Maori work), & it was possible to draw from that tribal experience by a process of "translation by composition," to bring new forms into our own language:

Zzzmmm 're lovely N nawu nnnn but some are & are
   at my howzes nahht bahyeenahtnwing but nawu
   nohwun baheegwing

& a hint here too of those occasions in which event precedes meaning.

In all of this there are two things, at least two, that have been operative for me: a fidelity to the past & a fidelity to the present; & the balance doesn't come easy or maybe, in any single instance, doesn't come at all. And a third thing, which I would be less than honest to disguise—that I've felt (in maybe all the anthologies but *Revolution of the Word*) a sense of the book as a poem, a large composition operating by assemblage or collage: my own voice emerging sometimes as translator, sometimes as commentator, but still obedient to the other voices, whether "out there" or "in here." In *A Big Jewish Book* I've carried it (or it's carried me) the furthest: a bigger space & less "my own" than *Poland/1931*, say, in which I was likewise using procedures like assemblage. . . .

The space is big enough to do it all, but in the end it isn't the idea of (so-called) "Jewishness" that most concerns me—rather a specific set of language plays, feats of word magic & language-centeredness (in its most profound sense) that come to a visible point within the illusion of the ethnically specific (the Indian in *Shaking the Pumpkin,* the Jewish here, etc.). What it brings me to in this one (the third of the volumes responding to *ethnos)* is a place where I can deal with the grapheme, the written word & image as such, which seems suddenly to be as primal as speech is—in the sense that all language doings are present in our first emergences as human beings.

Having gotten that far, I can now go back to the worlds of *Technicians* & *Pumpkin* & find it there also, can play with what intrigues me most in Derrida, that wild statement that "no reality or concept would correspond to the expression 'society without writing.'" The issue, then, has always been language—language & reality, nothing else—& the dichotomy of speaking & writing is, if no further specified, another con to keep us from our wholeness. Concerns like that—of language & wholeness—would seem to hold the work together; at least if you want a sense of where I think I'm going.

L=A=N=G=U=A=G=E, Number 8 (Volume 2, Number 2), June 1979.

From <u>TECHNICIANS OF THE SACRED</u> (1968)

The Poetics of Sound

TEXT: Dad a da da
           Dad a da da
           Dad a da da
           Da kata kai
      —Australian Aborigine wordless "rain chant"

COMMENTARY: Sounds only. No meaning, they say, in the words of the song, or no meaning you can get at by translation into-other-words; & yet it functions; the meaning contained then in how it's made to function. So here the key is in the "spell" & in the belief behind the "spell"—or in a whole system of beliefs, in magic, in the power of sound & breath & ritual to move an object toward ends determined by the poet-magus. Said the Navajo chanter (*hatali*) to Father Berard Haile: "The words have no meaning, but the song means, 'Take it, I give it to you.'"

Magic, then, is the first key & from this the idea of a special language or series of languages, extraordinary in their nature & effect, & uniting the user (through what Malinowski calls "the coefficient of weirdness") with the beings & things he's trying to influence or connect-with for a sharing of power, participation in a life beyond his own, beyond the human, etc.

Such special languages—meaningless &/or mysterious—are a small but nearly universal aspect of "primitive-&-archaic" poetry. They may involve (1) purely invented, meaningless sounds, (2) distortion of ordinary words & syntax, (3) ancient words emptied of their (long since forgotten) meanings, (4) words borrowed from other languages & likewise emptied. And all these may, in addition, be explained as (1) spirit language, (2) animal language, (3) ancestral language—distinctions between them often being blurred.

C. M. Bowra, in his book on "primitive song," wrongly views sound-poems like these as truly rudimentary, a kind of rock-bottom poetics. He writes that "since such (meaningless) sounds are easier to fit to music than intelligible sounds are . . . (they) look as if they were the earliest kind of song practiced by man." And yet this mantric use of sound is as close to (say) the Hindu *om* as to "purely" emotive sounds of the ay-ay-ay & yah-yah-yah variety. One could as well argue—at least where song is magic—that the use of words-emptied-of-meaning is a *late* development, even as geometric (abstract) art follows the naturalistic cows & bulls in the caves of Europe. The sound-poem has been brought to a high development in the Indian Americas, & its reappearance among some twentieth-century poets, European & American, is a further reminder that chronology isn't the question.

Namings

TEXTS: (1) The Upreared One.
Cat.
Terrible One.
Fat Face.
Turned Face.
The One Belonging to the Cobra.
   —Ancient Egyptian "god names"

(2) "Poetry is I say essentially a vocabulary just as prose is essentially not.

"And what is the vocabulary of which poetry absolutely is. It is a vocabulary based on the noun as prose is essentially and determinately and vigorously not based on the noun.

"Poetry is concerned with using with abusing, with losing with wanting, with denying with avoiding with adoring with replacing the noun. It is doing that always doing that, doing that and doing nothing but that. Poetry is doing nothing but using losing refusing and pleasing and betraying and caressing nouns.

". . . So that is poetry really loving the name of anything and that is not prose."

—G. Stein, *Lectures in America*

COMMENTARY: But the physicality of her description sticks: how she points to a material condition of poetry prior to verse or sequence, a way of thinking & feeling that treats words—all words—as substantive, measurable, having each a certain weight & extension, roots of words holding them firmly to earth, which the man cuts loose at will to let float up, then take root again so that their weights are again felt. And since the words are "real" (being measurable by weight & extension), they may be called-forth again or withheld, & being called-forth are the things called-forth? This is what the man believed once who made magic—"spells" & "charms" (carmina) being words in search of things. Measurable words as real as measurable things where both words & things are present in the naming. And the same tangible quality of words was felt whether they were spoken (that breath-entering-the-object Malinowski wrote of) or written or pictured or drummed. Something like that sensed then & there—rediscovered here & now.

Images

TEXTS: (1) *An Eskimo Poem for the Sun*
         The sun up there, up there.

         (2) *A Bushman Poem for the Blue Crane*
         A splinter of stone which is white.

COMMENTARY: Single-line poems, presented as such—in contrast to longer works that involve a linking of lines & images to make poems of greater complexity, showing development by image cluster, gaps in sequence, etc.

The poetry here is in song & image & word-play, but only the image comes near to translating itself enough to make a poem, or so the argument would go. What's happened, simply, is that something has been sighted & stated & set apart (by name or by description); given its own tune, too, to make it special; fixed, held fast in all this vanishing experience. It is this double sense of sighted/sited that represents the basic poetic function (a setting-apart-by-the-creation-of-special circumstances that the editor calls "sacralism") from which the rest follows—toward the building of more complicated structures & visions. But even here there is nothing naïve or minimal about the "sightings," save their clarity & the sense that, starting now, the plot (as Cage would say) is-going-to-thicken. Thickens, in fact, while we're watching; for the "single perception" of an image like a *splinter of stone/which is white* can as easily be sensed as two perceptions, & placed against the subject (*blue crane*) as two or three. But the decision has been made to voice it as a single line or musical phrase, & that decision itself is a statement about how we know things—& a choice.

Addenda. (1) The typical "primitive" song practice is to repeat (often also to distort) the one line indefinitely—or as long as the dance & ritual demand—then go on to a second song in the (ritual) sequence, a third, a fourth, etc. A turn in the ritual or dance would then represent something roughly equivalent to a strophe break, where a first series of single-line poems ends & a new, but related, series begins. This is utilized by the translators of works like the Australian *Djanggawul* & *Moon-Bone,* the African "praise poems," etc., who follow the "orders" of the ritual in their arrangement of single-line works into larger structures. Lines & series will often seem disconnected except that they're performed & happen together. The impact of this for our own time can't be ignored.

(2)   "Nothing of that, only an image—
      nothing else, utter oblivion—
      slanting through the words come vestiges of light!"
                          —Franz Kafka

(3) Ian Hamilton Finlay

OCEAN STRIPE SERIES

OCEAN STRIPE SERIES

~~the little sail of your name~~
the little sail of your name
~~the little sail of your name~~

Note. Each element in Finlay's poem appears on a separate page, broken lines in blue, words in red; thus color & the page boundary function with relation to his "single-image" as music does elsewhere. Thus, too, the further you get into it the less sense it makes to speak of a single-line poem—as in the "primitive" poems where any change in the music, even if the words remain unchanged, will alter the entire piece.

Bantu Combinations

TEXTS: (1) I am still carving an ironwood stick.
             I am still thinking about it.

        (2) The lake dries up at the edges.
             The elephant is killed by a small arrow.

COMMENTARY: Examples of plot-thickening in the area of "image": a conscious placing of image against image as though to see-what-happens. Apart from its presence in song, this juxtaposing of images turns up all over in the art, say, of the riddle—of which many of these Bantu "combinations" are, in fact, examples. Poem as opposition or balance of two or more images is also the basis of the haiku, less clearly of the sonnet. In all these the interest increases as the connection between the A & B sections becomes more & more strained, barely definable. Henri Junod, who transcribed these & others from the Bantu *circa* 1912, sensed this when he wrote:

> What makes a Bantu address especially interesting is . . . the *power of comparison* exhibited by Bantu speakers. . . . Sometimes the imagination is so subtle that the result is

almost incoherent. They are satisfied even if the point which the two things compared have in common . . . is almost infinitesimal.

Not subtlety, though, but *energy:* the power of word & image. For it's right here that the light breaks through most clearly; not the light of logic & simile, not even the flashing of a single image or name, but what feels "deeper" because further into it by now in the process of boxing myself into some corner, & to which (for the first time) the word "vision" might be said to apply.

Addenda. "The image cannot spring from any comparison but from the bringing together of two more or less remote realities. . . .

"The more distant and legitimate the relation between the two realities brought together, the stronger the image will be . . . the more emotive power and poetic reality it will possess."

—Pierre Reverdy

Aztec Definitions

TEXT: *The Precipice*

It is deep—a difficult, a dangerous place, a deathly place. It is dark, it is light. It is an abyss.

—*Florentine Codex*

COMMENTARY: [Fray Bernardino de Sahagún, a Franciscan monk, began in 1547—only twenty-six years after the fall of Mexico-Tenochtitlan—to compile documents in Nahuatl from Indian elders who repeated what they had learned by memory in their schools, the *calmécac* & the *telpochcalli*. These Nahuatl texts have been preserved in three codices, two in Madrid & one in Florence. In the eleventh book of the Florentine

149

codex—a kind of glossary of "earthly things"—the elders'
minds & words are drawn toward definitions of the most or-
dinary debris of their lives.]

For these men too there was a need to take a reckoning, to
see what things were left & to know them by the places in
which they could still be put. Something like that must have
been the case when the Friar, Sahagún, came to them, the
Conquest a few decades back & with it the smashing-to-hell of
previous certainties. What's to be done when the shape of
the real falls apart? If not to curse life, then to sense that life
returned to chaos is returned to the possibility of new thought.

Perhaps it only happened then—when they were powerless
—but more likely, from the work, they had known it before
& had welcomed it, this need to preserve the potency of the
real by a regular overturning & remaking of primary beliefs.
That archaic system, fixed in ritual & myth, had been wrenched
from them, but the pattern of it lingered: a habit of the
mind, in-grained but operating in no as yet recognizable new
context. What context did Sahagún give them? His work, writ-
ten largely in the Nahuatl of his informants, was the daybook
of a civilization that would die with the old men who were
helping him record it.

Everything goes but the words: the fragments of speech of a
people who had learned that the mind's grain is our final
clue to the real. He led them to a reconsideration, to an as-
semblage of "the things of New Spain"—of their gods, their
days, their signs & omens, their sacrifices, their songs, their
defeats, delivering to him, in the twelve books of his great
Codex, the first scientific epic of a civilization seen-as-it-
vanishes. But he doesn't drop it with the highstuff of culture,
for more astonishing than all that rich detail is how the habit
of their minds begins to play among the everyday debris. What
he must have asked them was to list & define the things-of-this-
world, all that we take most for granted. Here, though, the
mind finds release in a strange new encounter; free of ritual &
myth (The System) it approaches its objects as if for the first
time testing their existence. IT IS DARK, IT IS LIGHT: IT
IS WIDE-MOUTHED, IT IS NARROW-MOUTHED: all

of this said with no apparent sense of contradiction, as if, among these objects, the old pattern holds: of preparing chaos for the birth of something real.

Having come to this for ourselves, we can draw close to them, can hear in these "definitions" the sound of a poetry, a measure-by-placement-&-displacement, not far from our own. While their poetry proper—the songs & hymns collected by Sahagún & others—has its own goodness, it is as part of the fixed world before the upheaval, before the pattern was secularized & the eye freed. Only these definitions participate fully in that freedom, & this it seems to me is more important than whether they were intended as poems or not; for surely it should be clear by now that poetry is less literature than a process of thought & feeling & the arrangement of that into affective utterances. The conditions these definitions meet are the conditions of poetry.

Praise Poems / Assemblages

TEXT: Ogun kills on the right & destroys on the right
          Ogun kills on the left & destroys on the left
          Ogun kills suddenly in the house & suddenly in the field
          Ogun kills the child with the iron with which it plays
          Ogun kills in silence

                                        —(Yoruba)

COMMENTARY: The praise-poem (Yoruba *oriki,* Zulu *izibongo,* Basuto *lithoko,* etc.) turns up through much of Black Africa. At its simplest it's the stringing-together of a series of praise-names (usually independent utterances) describing the qualities owned by a particular man, god, animal, plant, place, etc. —anything, in short, that makes a "deep impression" on the singer. Often, too, it's not a question of "praise" but of delineation according to a certain method. The method itself is a kind of "collaging" from a fixed set of verses, lines & tags which are at the poet-diviner's disposal & can be supplemented by new invention. Among the Yoruba, e.g., each individual has a series of praise-names in the form of "descriptive phrases . . . that may be invented by relatives or neighbors or—most frequently —by the drummers" (thus: the translators Ulli Beier & Bakare Gbadamosi) or, particularly in the case of god names, may be handed down from the past. The actual singing (or drumming) of the praise-poem involves the arrangement of already existing materials into a new & coherent composition "having as its subject a single individual." The individual poet takes off from the work of the collectivity, to which he adds as last in a line of makers. But his "art" is one of assemblage—the weighing of line against line.

The Poetics of Chance (I): "The Book of Changes"

TEXT: The Clinging is fire, the sun, lightning, the middle daughter.

It means coats of mail & helmets; it means lances & weapons. Among men it means the big-bellied.

. . . .

Keeping Still is the mountain; it is a bypath; it means little stones, doors & openings, fruits & seeds, eunuchs & watchmen, the fingers; it is the dog, the rat, & the various kinds of blackbilled birds.

—*I Ching* ("The Book of Changes")

COMMENTARY: The *I Ching*, which some have dated as far back as 2000 B.C. (& if not that old is, anyway, very ancient), is the basis in China for the kind of thought that sees life & development as a working-out or constant reshuffling of contrary forces; or, as Blake had it:

without contraries is no progression;
reason & energy, love & hate, good & evil,
are all necessary to human existence.

While the "practical" side of the *I Ching* deals with divination by yarrow sticks, etc., some sections, like the one given here, show a developed ability to think-in-images, to place name against name, quality against quality, while retaining that passion for the names of things that Gertrude Stein saw as the basis of all poetry. Partly it's a question of resemblances & analogy, but at this point in where "we" are, what's of still greater importance is the possibility of a kind of tension, energy, etc., generated by the joining of disparate, even arbitrary, images. *Observation:* Every new correspondence acts on its subject, which it changes, & on the entire field; every change a measurable burst of energy. *Questions:* Is the correspondence *there,* is it imposed, & does it finally matter? If the common term "hot" or "dry" links "fire" with "the sun, the lightning, the upper part of the trunk," what links it with "big-bellied" or "lances & weapons"? What common quality "justifies" the linking of nouns in the "keeping still" series, & if you find one (Confucius did!) are you gaining consistency through a loss of power? The editor can only witness to his sense of this series of "correspondences" being a handy ancient manual of poetic process (of *all* those levels of vision Blake spoke of)—& values it as such.

Wrote Carl Jung in the foreword to Wilhelm's translation of the *I Ching:* "The manner in which the *I Ching* tends to look upon reality seems to disfavor our causalistic procedures. The moment under actual observation appears to the ancient Chinese view more of a chance hit than a clearly defined result of concurring causal chain processes. The matter of interest seems to be the configuration formed by chance events in the moment of observation, & not at all the hypothetical reasons that seemingly account for the coincidence."

Thought of this kind, when applied to the field-of-the-poem, defines that field both in primitive/archaic & in much modern poetry: that whatever falls within the same space determines the meaning of that space. What Jung called "synchronicity" (with the problems it raises of indeterminacy & the observer's part in structuring the real) becomes a principle of composition: common link between such otherwise different modes as chance poetry, automatic writing, "deep" image, collage, projective verse, etc., & between those & the whole world of non-sequential & non-causal thought. That modern physics at the same time moves closer to a situation in which anything-can-happen, is of interest too in any consideration of where we presently are.

The Poetics of Chance (II): "The Praises of the Falls"

TEXT: *The Lamp of the Seers*

> The angry man
> fights with his mother-in-law
>
> What was the good of those lamps?
>
> Seeing wonders
> every morning
> your sins passed by
>
> & you saw them
> & saw the child of a cow
> & of a human being
>
> saw them, could tell them
> apart
>
> from the entrails
>   —Basuto "Praises of the Falls"

COMMENTARY: "Praises" like these—first gathered by the Basuto writer Joas Mapetla—accompany the casting of oracle bones. Their purpose is:

(1) to create, as with music, the conditions under which the bones are to be read, i.e., to provide that "coefficient of weirdness" Malinowski spoke of [see above, p. 144] in which the words *are* music, act upon us before their sense is clear or against the possibility of any fixed meaning;

(2) as open-ended imagery that can then—almost "falsely" —be read as secret closed statements (the functional language of the oracle) in the participants' search for clues to the unknown: the cause of disease & misfortune, etc.

Mapetla's description of the bones & the procedures for casting is never clear. There are apparently four to twenty in a set or "litaola": four principal ones from the hoofs & horns of oxen, with lesser bones from ankles & hindlegs of anteaters, springbok, sheep, goats, monkeys, also occasional shells, twigs & stones. The four major bones are designated as greater & lesser male & greater & lesser female, & are read according to the sides on which they fall, direction of fall, positions relative to each other & to the minor bones, etc. The greater male & female have four sides called walking, standing, covering, & dying; the lesser male & female only walking & dying.

Unlike the typical African praise poem, in which the lines or praises are independent units that the poet brings together in a kind of collage, it is the fall of the bones that here suggests what lines or praises will be used & determines their order. Thus chance—to a greater or lesser degree—serves to program the divining praises much as dice-castings, tarot-readings, random digit tables, etc., take on a structuring & selecting function for some contemporary poets & artists. In both cases, syntactical devices may be used to bridge the lines, or the disjunction between lines (as silence or punctuation) may be accepted on its own.

Widespread throughout Africa, such divinatory/chance procedures form a body of lore & poetry that, carefully assembled, may represent an African *I Ching* or *Book of Changes*.

Technicians of the Sacred. Extended commentary on "Aztec Definitions," from *Some/thing*, Volume 1, Number 1, Spring 1965.

THE POETRY OF NUMBER (1977)

I was drawn back—while in the process of constructing *A Big Jewish Book,* the "gematria" (numerology) sections in particular—to a consideration of number as it enters our works & lives. A "poetry of number" (& for the Jews all letters of the alphabet were numbers, each page a field of numbers) was once the limit of the poetry we could see, not only that "numbers" was itself the working term for "verse," but that it linked *all* arts & sciences together: a great unifying & synthesizing concept with roots into the Orphic-based, inspired & sacred mathematics of the Pythagoreans. Wrote Aristotle, who was no way at ease with it:

> The Pythagoreans were . . . the first to take up mathematics . . . & thought its principles were the principles of all things. . . . Since they saw that the modifications & ratios of the musical scales were expressible in number; since, then, all other things in their whole nature seemed to be modeled on numbers, & numbers seemed to be the first things in the whole of nature, they supposed the elements of all things, & the whole heaven to be a musical scale & number.

And above their heads the stars grouped themselves into letters, numbers, appearing thus to the literate but still luny wanderer of the *Zohar,* he who looked out to the east, there saw "something like letters marching in the sky, some rising, others descending. These brilliant characters. . . the letters—numbers—with which God has formed heaven & earth."

In our own time too there are poets & artists who generate works by numbers (however changed the number theories are), who celebrate numbers, or who see measure ("measure, number & weight") not as a literary device merely but a particular "stance toward reality" These open new ways for us or, in scanning again the human past, lead to a more far-ranging sense of structure than did our conventional metrics, which also had its source there, though in a notion, now behind us, of the finite & the fixed—of *perfect* numbers. Writes Eric Mottram: "The poetry of numerology is part of the long dialectic of freedom & necessity. . . . There is nothing slavish, degrading or anti-human in it, unless used as a limited imposition of geometry as the model of a State. Anarchism balances between chance & necessity, as nature does. The totalitarian state, simply, is not total but partial, an imposition of insane reason."

For myself the numbers have been a presence beneath speech, but I have known them also, being Jewish, in the letters of the alphabet I work with. My father drew them with his finger on the kitchen table. And I have lain awake like him & counted numbers in sequences that play on mind & body until the rhythm of numbers, letters, shapes, & forms is inescapable—as still another source of naming.

New Wilderness Letter, Volume 1, Number 2, July–August 1977.

GEMATRIA (1978)

Gematria is the general term for a variety of traditional coding practices used by the Jewish mystic-poets to establish correspondences between words or series of words based on the numerical equivalence of the sums of their letters or on the interchange of letters according to a set system. The numerical method—*gematria* per se—typically took *alef* as 1, *bet* as 2, *yod* as 10, *kuf* as 100, etc., through *tav* (last letter) as 400—although more complicated methods (e.g., reduction to single digits, etc.) were later introduced. Non-numerical methods included: (1) anagrams, or rearrangements of the letters of a word to form a new word or word series, as "god" to "dog" in English; (2) *notarikon,* the derivation of a new word from the initial letters of several others & vice versa, as "god," say, from "garden of delight"; & (3) *temura,* various systems of letter code, e.g., the common one in which the first half of the alphabet is placed over the second & letters are substituted between the resultant rows, etc., *in search of meaningful combinations.*

Processes of this kind go back to Greek, even Babylonian, practice, & early enter the rabbinic literature. But the greatest development was among kabbalists from the twelfth century on, who used it both to discover divine & angelic names & to uncover correspondences between ideas & images by means free of subjective interference. When set out as poems, the resemblance of the *gematria* to a poetry of correspondences in our own time is evident, as also to instances of process poetry & art based on (more or less) mechanical formulas for the generation of both simple & extended series of permutations & combinations. Thus, Jackson Mac Low's "vocabularies," in which the text (or score) "is a drawing, painting or collage consisting of all the words I can think of (or fit on the paper or canvas) spelled solely with the letters of one person's name," are very close in method—even, ultimately, in intention—to the first non-numerical process described above.

While numerical *gematria* & coded *temura* come easily in a language like Hebrew which is written without vowels, the possibility of similar workings in English shouldn't be discounted. *Gematria*-generated poems can also be composed by translation from Hebrew; thus,

Messiah

Snake.

The Soul of Adam

Lilith.

The Garden

Shadow.
Stone.
The Brain.

The fact of translation may, in fact, add to the apparent "distance & power" of the combinations, a direct relationship that twentieth-century poets like Reverdy saw as the basis of the poetic image. [See above, page 149.]

A Big Jewish Book.

ABRAHAM ABULAFIA (1978)

Abraham Abulafia (1240–*c*.1291) was a mystic & poet, whose poetry of permutations (a kind of medieval "lettrism" he called The Path of Names) took at its most complex the form of nearly 200 mandalic circles, consisting of a discourse on meditation, a set of instructions for specific permutations, & the permutations of the letters themselves. In his *Book of Circles* (one name for it; the other was *The Life of the World to Come)*, the permutations work off the so-called Name-of-72: i.e., 72 three-letter syllables "based on the three verses of Exodus 14:19–21, each of which contains 72 letters. . . . It was made up by joining the first letter of verse 19, the last letter of 20, and the first of 21, to form its first triad: the second letter of 19, the penultimate of 20, and the second of 21, to make the second triad, and so on until we have 72 three-letter terms comprising all the letters of these verses." (J. Trachtenberg, *Jewish Magic & Superstition*) Abulafia in turn arranges the syllables in rows & columns, then sets them into circles according to instructions ("middle of the first, middle of the last," etc.), which form part of the circles as well. In this way the disciple is led into the circles, must follow their message as an act of concentration.

Abulafia himself writes of the abstracting/spiritualizing process which he then employs & by which the world is apprehended as language/sound: "Know that the method of *tseruf* (the combination of letters) can be compared to music; for the ear hears sounds from various combinations, in accordance with the character of the melody & the instrument. Also, two different instruments can form a combination, & if the sounds combine, the listener's ear registers a pleasant sensation in acknowledging their difference. . . . The same is true of the combination of letters. It touches the first string, which is comparable to the first letters, & proceeds to the second, third, fourth, & fifth, & the various sounds combine. And the secrets, which express themselves in these combinations, delight the heart which acknowledges its God & is filled with ever fresh joy." Thus the letters—by a process called *dilug* (skipping)—become a basis for meditation "on the essence of one's thought, abstracting from it every word, be it connected with a notion or not . . . (by putting) the consonants which one is combining into swift motion." For Abulafia & others, such processes remain essentially "oral," in the sense of open-ended: an improvisatory meditation on a fixed base (torah, names of God, etc.) whose true meanings are not "literal" but the occasion for an ongoing process of reconstruction (revelation) & sounding. In touch with yogic currents from the East, Abulafia's intention here seems clearly mantric; but his practice of a systemic & concrete poetry also closely resembles the twentieth-century lettrism of Isidore Isou, the asymmetries & nuclei of Jackson Mac Low, & the blues kabbala improvisations of Jack Hirschman, all of whom he may have influenced.

Legends about Abulafia—buttressed by a pseudo-autobiography—tell how he adopted the name of the angel Raziel, went as messiah to interrogate the pope, was arrested & condemned to die, & only escaped after the pope's own death. A model, therefore, of the poet/rebel in language & in life, common to Jewish & other marginalities within the monolithic nation-state.

A Big Jewish Book.

AT THE BOUNDARIES (1978)

The mind, in the *poesis* of kabbala, strove toward the *Ein Sof,* the "endless," "limitless," or this: the basic proposition of the search: for what is out of reach, unknowable: the secret of the Jewish mysteries that strains the powers of a language. Here the poetry is in the telling, *is* the telling: the account through language, by whatever means, to approach the secret by its outer forms: as rays, as emanations, as bodies, as images, as sounds, as words, as names. But the process thus stated is doomed to fail, for the *Ein Sof,* writes Gershom Scholem, is "not accessible even to the innermost thought of the contemplative," rather "a term or image signifying the domain of the hidden God that lies beyond any impulse toward creation." As one instance this leads to that (gnostic) dualism in which our world becomes, exists, in separation as the creation of a second force completely evil. Otherwise, as in all *poesis* at the boundaries, the limitless ("beyond all thought") is that to which all thought somehow returns as source. Not the "unknown," a simpler proposition, but the "unknowable." "Cause of all causes." Or again: "Root of all roots."

A Big Jewish Book.

SOUNDING EVENTS (1978)

Sound the words as quickly as possible
Sound the words as loudly as possible
Sound the words in a whisper

Sound the words while jumping in place
Sound the words while beating your chest
Sound the words while swaying sideways

Sound the words while clapping hands
Sound the words while turning somersaults
Sound the words while standing still

Sound the words a second time
Sound the words a third time
Sound the words a fourth time

Sound the words a fifth time
Sound the words a sixth time
Sound the words a seventh time

Sound the words an eighth time
Sound the words a ninth time
Sound the words a tenth time

Sound the words a hundred times
Sound the words a thousand times
Sound the words in silence

COMMENTARY: Examples in the Jewish tradition of ways in which the written text (as prayer or meditation/mantra) was brought back to the world of sound & gesture.

(1) "You will meet a company of seers coming down from the high place with a psaltery, a tambourine, a pipe, & a harp;

& they will prophesy: & the spirit of Yahveh will come upon you, & you will prophesy with them, & will be turned into another man." (I Samuel 10:5–6)

(2) "Prayer is copulation with the Shekinah. Just as there is swaying when copulation begins so, too, a man must sway at first & then he can remain immobile & attached to the Shekinah with great attachment. As a result of his swaying a man is able to attain a powerful stage of arousal. For he will ask himself: Why do I sway my body? Presumably it is because the Shekinah stands over against me. And as a result he will attain to a stage of great enthusiasm." (From *Tsava'at ha-Ribash*, quoted in L. Jacobs, *Hasidic Prayer.*)

(3) "He who reads without melody & repeats without song, concerning him the Scripture says: Therefore I also gave them statutes which were not to their advantage." (Rabbi Yohanan ben Zakkai, Talmud: *Megila* 32a.)

A Big Jewish Book.

NEW MODELS, NEW VISIONS: SOME NOTES TOWARD A POETICS OF PERFORMANCE (1977)

The fact of performance now runs through all our arts, and the arts themselves begin to merge and lose their old distinctions, till it's apparent that we're no longer where we were to start with. The Renaissance is over or it begins again with us. Yet the origins we seek—the frame that bounds our past, that's set against an open-ended future—are no longer Greek, nor even Indo-European, but take in all times and places. To say this isn't to deny history, for we're in fact involved with history, with the sense of ourselves "in time" and in relation to other forms of human experience besides our own. The model —or better, the vision—has shifted: away from a "great tradition" centered in a single stream of art and literature in the West, to a *greater* tradition that includes, sometimes as its central fact, preliterate and oral cultures throughout the world, with a sense of their connection to subterranean but literate traditions in civilizations both East and West. "Thought is made in the mouth," said Tristan Tzara, and Edmond Jabès: "The book is as old as fire and water"—and both, we know, are right.

The change of view, for those who have experienced it, is by now virtually paradigmatic. We live with it in practice and find it more and more difficult to communicate with those who still work with the older paradigm. Thus, what appears to us as essentially creative—how can we doubt it?— carries for others the threat that was inherent when Tzara, as arch Dadaist, called *circa* 1917, for "a great negative work of destruction" against a late, overly textualized derivation from the Renaissance paradigm of culture and history. No longer viable, that great Western thesis was already synthesizing, setting the stage for its own disappearance. The other side of Tzara's work—and increasingly that of other artists within the several avant-gardes, the different, often conflicted sides of "modernism"—was, we now see clearly, a great positive work of construction/synthesis. With Tzara it took the form of a projected anthology, *Poèmes nègres,* a gathering of African and Oceanic poems culled from existing ethnographies and chanted at Dada performances in Zurich's Cabaret Voltaire. To the older brokers of taste—the bearers of Western values in an age of chaos—this may have looked like yet another Dada gag, but seeing it now in its actual publication six decades after the fact, it reads like a first, almost too serious attempt at a new classic anthology. In circulation orally, it formed with Tzara's own poetry—the process of a life and its emergence as performance in the soundworks and simultaneities of the dada soirées, etc.—one of the prophetic statements of where our work was to go.

Sixty years after Dada, a wide range of artists have been making deliberate and increasing use of ritual models for performance, have swept up arts like painting, sculpture, poetry (if those terms still apply) long separated from their origins in performance. (Traditional performance arts—music, theater, dance—have undergone similarly extreme transformations: often, like the others, toward a virtual liberation from the dominance of text.) The principal function here may be viewed as that of mapping and exploration, but however defined or simplified (text, e.g., doesn't vanish but is revialized; so, likewise, the Greco-European past itself), the performance/ritual impulse seems clear throughout: in "happenings" and related event pieces (particularly those that involve participatory performance), in meditative works (often on an explicitly mantric model), in earthworks (derived from monumental American Indian structures), in dreamworks that play off trance and ecstasy, in bodyworks (including acts of self-mutilation and endurance that seem to test the model), in a range of healing events as literal explorations of the shamanistic premise, in animal language pieces related to the new ethology, etc.*

* When I made a similar point in *Technicians of the Sacred* ten years earlier, I attributed the relation between "primitive" ritual and contemporary art and performance to an implicit coincidence of attitudes, where today the relation seems up-front, explicit, and increasingly comparable to the Greek and Roman model in Renaissance Europe, the

●

While a likely characteristic of the new paradigm is an overt disdain for paradigms *per se,* it seems altogether possible to state a number of going assumptions as these relate to performance. I won't try to sort them out but will simply present them for consideration in the order in which they come to mind.

(1) There is a strong sense of continuities, already alluded to, within the total range of human cultures and arts, and a sense as well that the drive toward performance goes back to our pre-human biological inheritance—that performance and culture, even language, precede the actual emergence of the species: hence an ethological continuity as well. With this comes a rejection of the idea of artistic "progress" and a tendency to link avant-garde and "traditional" performance (tribal/oral, archaic, etc.) as forms of what Richard Schechner calls *transformational* theater and art—in opposition to the "mimetic/re-actualizing" art of the older paradigm.

(2) There is an unquestionable and far-reaching breakdown of boundaries and genres: between "art and life" (Cage, Kaprow), between various conventionally defined arts (intermedia and performance art, concrete poetry), and between arts and non-arts *(musique concrete,* found art, etc.). The consequences here are immense, and I'll only give a few, perhaps too obvious, examples (ideas of this kind do in fact relate to much else that is stated in these pages):

—that social conflicts are a form of theater (V. Turner) and that organized theater may be an arena for the projection and/or stimulation of social conflict;

—that art has again recognized itself as visionary, and that there may be no useful distinction between vision-as-vision and vision-as-art (thus, too, the idea in common between Freud and the Surrealists, that the dream is a dream-*work,* i.e., a work-of-art);

Chinese model in medieval Japan, the Toltec model among the Aztecs, etc.: i.e., an overt influence but alive enough to work a series of distortions conditioned by the later culture and symptomatic of the obvious differences between the two.

—that there is a continuum, rather than a barrier, between music and noise; between poetry and prose (the language of inspiration and the language of common and special discourse); between dance and normal locomotion (walking, running, jumping), etc.;

—that there is no hierarchy of media in the visual arts, no hierarchy of instrumentation in music, and that qualitative distinctions between high and low genres and modes (opera and vaudeville, high rhetoric and slang) are no longer operational;

—that neither advanced technology (electronically produced sound and image, etc.) nor hypothetically primitive devices (pulse and breath, the sound of rock on rock, of hand on water) are closed off to the artist willing to employ them.

The action hereafter is "between" and "among," the forms hybrid and vigorous and pushing always toward an actual and new completeness. Here is the surfacing, resurfacing in fact of that "liminality" that Victor Turner recognizes rightly as the place of "fruitful chaos" and possibility—but no less "here" than "there." It is, to say it quickly, the consequence in art-and-life of the freeing-up of the "dialectical imagination."

(3) There is a move away from the idea of "masterpiece" to one of the transientness and self-obsolescence of the art-work. The work past its moment becomes a document (mere history), and the artist becomes, increasingly, the surviving non-specialist in an age of technocracy.

(4) From this there follows a new sense of function in art, in which the value of a work isn't inherent in its formal or aesthetic characteristics—its shape or its complexity or simplicity as an object—but in what it does, or what the artist or his surrogate does with it, how he performs it in a given context. This is different in turn from the other, equally functional concept of art as propaganda, at least insofar as the latter forces the artist to repeat "truths" already known, etc., in the service of the total state. As an example of a nonformal, functional approach to the are object as instrument-of-

power, take the following, from my conversations with the Seneca Indian sculptor/carver, Avery Jimerson:

I told him that I thought Floyd John's mask was very beautiful, but he said it wasn't because it didn't have real power [the power, for example, to handle burning coals while wearing it]. His own father had had a mask that did, until there was a fire in his house and it was burnt to ashes. But his father could still see the features of the mask and so, before it crumbled, he hurried out and carved a second mask. And that second mask looked like the first in every detail. Only it had no power. (J. R., *A Seneca Journal*)

(5) There follows further, in the contemporary instance, a stress on action and/or process. Accordingly the performance or ritual model includes the act of composition itself: the artist's life as an unfolding through his performance of it. (The consideration of this private or closed side of performance is a little like Richard Schechner's discovery that rehearsal/preparation is a theatrical/ritual event as important as the showing it precedes.) Signs of the artist's or poet's presence are demanded in the published work, and in our own time this has come increasingly to take the form of his or her performance of that work, unfolding it or testifying to it in a public place. The personal presence is an instance as well of localization, of a growing concern with particular and local definitions; for what, asks David Antin, can be more local than the person?

(6) Along with the artist, the audience enters the performance arena as participant—or, the audience "disappears" as the distinction between doer and viewer, like the other distinctions mentioned herein, begins to blur. For this the tribal/oral is a particularly clear model, often referred to by the creators of 1960s happenings and the theatrical pieces that invited, even coerced, audience participation toward an ultimate democratizing of the arts. In a more general way, many artists have come to see themselves as essentially the initiators of the work ("makers of the plot but not of everything that enters into the plot"—Jackson Mac Low), expanding the art process

by inviting the audience to join them in an act of "co-creation" or to respond with a new work in which the one-time viewer/listener himself becomes the maker. The response-as-creation thus supercedes the response-as-criticism, just as the maker/particularizer comes to be viewed (or to view himself) as the superior of the interpreter/generalizer. It is this which Charles Olson had in mind when he saw us emerging from a "generalizing time," etc., to regain a sense of the poem "as the act of the instant . . . not the act of thought about the instant." [See above, page 10.] More dramatically, as a contrast between the involved participant and the objective observer, it turns up in Gary Snyder's story of Alfred Kroeber and his Mojave informant, *circa* 1902, in which Kroeber sits through six days of intense oral narration, the story of the world from its beginnings, and then writes:

> When our sixth day ended he still again said another day would see us through. But by then I was overdue at Berkeley. And as the prospective day might once more have stretched into several, I reluctantly broke off, promising him and myself that I would return to Needles when I could, not later than next winter, to conclude recording the tale. By next winter Inyo-Kutavere had died, and the tale thus remains unfinished. . . . He was stone blind. He was below the average of Mojave tallness, slight in figure, spare, almost frail with age, his gray hair long and unkempt, his features sharp, delicate, sensitive. . . . He sat indoors on the loose sand floor of the house for the whole of the six days that I was with him in the frequent posture of Mojave men, his feet beneath him or behind him to the side, not with legs crossed. He sat still but smoked all the Sweet Caporal cigarettes I provided. His house mates sat around and listened or went and came as they had things to do.

To which Snyder adds the single sentence: "That old man sitting in the sand house telling his story is who we must become—not A. L. Kroeber, as fine as he was."

The model switch is here apparent. But in addition the poet-as-informant stands in the same relation to those who speak of poetry or art from outside the sphere of its making as do any of the world's aboriginals. The antagonism to literature and to criticism is, for the poet and artist, no different from that to anthropology, say, on the part of the Native American militant. It is a question in short of the right to self-definition.

(7) There is an increasing use of real time, extended time, etc., and/or a blurring of the distinction between those and theatrical time, in line with the transformative view of the "work" as a process that's really happening. (Analogues to this, as alternative modes of narration, performance, etc., are again sought in tribal/oral rituals.) In addition an area of performance using similarly extended time techniques toward actual transformations (of the self, of consciousness, etc.) parallels that of traditional meditation (*mantra, yantra,* in the Tantric context), thus an exploration of the boundaries of mind that Snyder offers as the central work of contemporary man, or Duchamp from a perspective not all that different: "to put art again at the service of mind."

●

For all of this recognition of cultural origins and particularities, the crunch, the paradox, is that the place, if not the stance, of the artist and poet is increasingly beyond culture—a characteristic, inevitably, of biospheric societies. Imperialistic in their earlier forms and based on a paradigm of "the dominant culture" (principally the noble/imperial myths of "Western civilization" and of "progress," etc. on a Western or European model), these have in their *avant-garde* phase been turning to the "symposium of the whole" projected by Robert Duncan. [See above, page 119.] More strongly felt in the industrial and capitalist west, this may be the last move of its kind still to be initiated by the Euro-Americans: a recognition of the new/old order in which the whole is equal to but no greater than the works of all its parts.

Performance in Postmodern Culture, edited by Michel Benamou & Charles Caramello (Coda Press, 1977). This is a version of an essay presented at the Wenner-Gren Foundation symposium, "Cultural Frames & Reflections: Ritual, Drama & Spectacle," held in Burg Wartenstein, Austria, August 27–September 5, 1977.

4 / Beyond Poetics

So, something more than literature is going on here: for our-selves . . . the question of how the concepts & techniques of the "sacred" can persist in the "secular" world.

AN ACADEMIC PROPOSAL (1972)

For a period of twenty-five years, say, or as long as it takes a new generation to discover where it lives, take the great Greek epics out of the undergraduate curricula, & replace them with the great American epics. Study the *Popol Vuh* where you now study Homer, & study Homer where you now study the *Popol Vuh*—as exotic anthropology, etc. If you have a place in your mind for the *Greek Anthology* (God knows you may not), let it be filled by Astrov's *Winged Serpent* or the present editor's *Technicians of the Sacred* or this very volume you are reading. Teach courses in religion that begin: "This is the account of how all was in suspense, all calm, in silence; all motionless, still, & the expanse of the sky was empty"—& use this as a norm with which to compare all other religious books, whether Greek or Hebrew. Encourage poets to translate the native American classics (a new version for each new generation), but first teach them how to sing. Let young Indian poets (who still can sing or tell-a-story) teach young White poets to do so. Establish chairs in American literature & theology, etc. to be filled by men trained in the oral transmission. Remember, too, that the old singers & narrators are still alive (or that their sons & grandsons are), & that to despise them or leave them in poverty is an outrage against the spirit-of-the-land. Call this outrage the sin-against-Homer.

Teach courses with a rattle & a drum.

Shaking the Pumpkin.

INDIANS & WILDERNESS (1979)

We are by now—in those places where most of us live who carry on the discourse about "wilderness"—fairly settled as to what that discourse is about. Wilderness is where we don't live habitually & where we do "return" deliberately. We have forgotten it, we say, & have to learn again to live with it. It is what survives apart from those of us who live, habitually, outside it: Wordworth's "Nature" that "never did betray the heart that loved her": a living world, that part of it in which the human doesn't dominate. If it has its people, human inhabitants who live in it habitually, then they themselves are people ("two-leggeds" in the lingo of the Sioux) living in a "state of nature," outside the state as state or *polis*. In America they are (or were) the native peoples/nature peoples: Indians.

So it goes, this widespread idea that connects Indians with wilderness. Whites have it to a fault; Indians raise it often in a different sense. A typical Indian strategy is to say of "Indian & wilderness": *The Whites came here & looked at the continent & said: This is something different, this is wilderness. The Indians said: This is home.* At home on the continent, the land, they said, & we do too. But that can mean at least two things: that the Indian is or was at home in "wilderness" & that "wilderness" therefore equals "home"; or that the Indian makes or made a distinction between his habitation & the surrounding non-habitation, which the Whites fail or failed to honor, treating the whole continent in its aboriginal pre-White state as a continuous "wilderness."

I would like to discuss my own readings of these propositions, which have led me to two not mutually exclusive conclusions: that most—but not necessarily all—aboriginal American peoples lived in a relation to their natural environment clearly different from that prevailing in seventeenth-century Europe; and that most—but not necessarily all—aboriginal American peoples made the normal human distinction between the settled & socialized condition in which they lived & the other-than-human, natural & often terrifying condition in which they did not live but into which they ventured for refreshment, adventure & power. In other words, the nature-culture distinction so beloved of anthropologists—the "raw" & the "cooked" as borrowed by Lévi-Strauss from Native American usage—is a part of human consciousness everywhere. It unites Indian & anthropologist in a common separation from—& not so common aspiration to return to—*wildness*.

That much is basic anthropology, in no sense surprising. What is more startling is to discover that no settled human culture is uncomplicatedly "at home" in wilderness or fails to make the wilderness distinction—unless of course it ceases to be that untamed thing that haunts us & becomes a giant & neatly boundaried public park.

●

The word itself—"wilderness"—is by now a part of the common American coinage. As such it conjures up an image of rich & untamed nature, a remnant paradise still free from human cultivation. "Wildness" & "be*wilder*ment" are its cognates, & behind them "wold" or "*wood*land," which was also Middle English jive for "madness," "wilderness of the mind." (Possibly also "world" itself as total wilderness.) It is a configuration different from the French, say, which conventionally translated "wilderness" as *désert*, i.e. a wasteland, a solitude; uninhabited, unfrequented, dead, & certainly uncultivated: in brief, the English "desert." It is a usage much harsher than our own, although our own usage ("wilderness") once was harsh enough to translate the many Hebrew words for "desert" ("the voice of one crying in the wilderness," etc.).

But American views of "desert" have also mellowed, as in the pop image of Disney's *Living Desert;* and the deserts of California, like the nearby mountain woodlands, have become great all-purpose recreation areas. To get at this sense of a benign "wilderness," the French *nature*—although it doesn't turn up in older dictionaries as a suggested term—seems possible if much too broad or much too reminiscent of its nineteenth-century usage. *Sauvagerie,* as "wildness," applies not to the place but to the people of the wilderness—literally the "savages" or "forest people," also called *les naturels* or *les natifs* (the "natives").

To the first Europeans in America, the idea of "wilderness," like that of "desert," was harsh & terrifying: not a place empty of life but empty of the social & religious order they thought of as defining their own state. All America was one vast "wilderness," a "desert" from their point of view as farmers & exploiters. Uncultivated land yet thick with life; that much was inescapable & even more threatening (thereby alluring) than the other "desert" would have been. Fecund, prolific, sexual, out of the grasp of "Man" & "God": "the realm of Nature under Satan's control," wrote one of them, echoing the basic Western-Christian view. It was nature watched from behind the wall of city or farmyard by those fearing & opposing whatever was outside. And there was a mental wall also, a wall against the inner savagery, the untamed parts of consciousness: dream & sexuality, unconscious & subconscious posited as real but placed in exile, banished under Christian law. These were also in "the realm of Nature under Satan's control."

In that spirit America would be remade as a great walled city: the Heavenly City of the Puritans, the New Jerusalem. They set out to conquer the Wilderness, to subdue & above all to cultivate it (by the sweat of their brows, the Bible told them) as central to the business of their lives. And its inhabitants also: "wilderness people" whom you could exploit & hate as something less than human (if not positively satanic) or exploit & love or envy as noble children, "savages" who lived without the corruptions of "civilization."

But even so you conquered them & IT: the Great American Desert: a threat to overcome. The terms of the discourse only made it more simple.

●

Who were the "wilderness people" so defined, & what were they apart from their European definition?

North of Mexico they were mostly small nations, independent groups living in village settlements &/or established hunting areas. They were, in a term introduced into the "ethnopoetic" vocabulary by Gary Snyder, "eco-system people": "societies"—he writes after Ray Dasmann—"whose life and economies are centered in terms of natural regions and watersheds, as against those ['biospheric cultures'] who discovered—seven or eight thousand years ago in a few corners of the globe—that it was 'profitable' to spill over into another drainage, another watershed, another people's territory, and steal away its resources, natural or human." In itself that's accurate enough, deceptive only to those who jump to conclude—by a cliché of pseudo-anthropology—that Indians were mostly hunters & gatherers. Hunters they largely remained—for protein subsistence, etc.—but for the greater part, they were agriculturists, whose farming needs defined places of cultivation & residence to be set aside as "home land."

(That much is absolutely crucial to an understanding of the deception involved in European claims to territorial rights based on the prerogatives of "civilization" over uncultivated "savagery." Even hunters & gatherers—the fishing nations of the Northwest an extreme example—lived a more settled life than popularly imagined, with a clear distinction between "home" & "wilderness.")

Insofar as Indians remained eco-system people & subsistence hunters (& in Meso-America they did in fact make the jump to a form of biospheric imperialism), they were "close to nature." They related to Earth—nature up close—as home & mother, & to other species as kin & guardians. Whether they resisted farming entirely ("I will not plow my mother's breast"—Smohalla) or practiced it within their own domain, the other-than-human entered their consciousness in many ways & kept a check on the human. (This much they had in common with other gatherers & low-technology farmers.) As hunters they kept a knowledge of wild animals, & in their "hunting magic" a feeling of connection & responsibility, while as farmers & settled folk—more simply as human beings—they knew themselves as a species apart, whose culture made them different. They felt—at least through their shaman-poets—that they could speak the language of animals & gods, & through that language they journeyed from the settled place & found the wilderness beyond society & culture, & in their minds as well.

It is a different configuration from that of Europe, which at one point reached the most extreme form of alienation from outer & inner nature: demonic, fenced off, kept at bay. The European night sky (& that of European America as well) vanished in the murky light of cities, and the land beyond the cities was entered at great risk for rape & exploitation. Animals were brought within the city or (soulless, dangerous) were hunted down & consciously wiped out. Men had entered on a state of war with nature.

The Indians by contrast—at least outside of Mexico—didn't take the separation as absolute & moral. Through a series of crossovers into wilderness—for subsistence, recreation—they developed a sense of ecological balance & maintained it through millennia of observation (& some notable failures & warnings: species extinctions, etc.), contributing to later America the idea, in Snyder's classic formulation, that " 'Nature' means wilderness, the untamed realm of total freedom, not brutish and nasty, but *beautiful* and *terrible*." (Italics mine.—J. R.)

Both terms are crucial, & both (as contrary aspects of a single dialectic) are best pursued by example.

●

The mental set of hunters permeates the first poetry of America: at its broadest a call to other beings to leave the deeper wilderness (domain beyond the human) & be present for the hunt:

You dear little orphan
creep out of the water
panting on this beautiful shore,
puh, puh, like this, puh, puh,
O welcome gift
in the shape of a seal!
        (Eskimo)

Or to be present for the medicine rite & feast, often their gift as well:

    the crows came in
    the crows sat down
            (Seneca)

—not only animals but other power forms (raw beings) also:

    I am making
        a wind come here

        it's coming
                (Crow)

The care in observation & the empathy are visible:

    The whale coming to shore is sick
    the sharks have eaten her bowels
    & the meat of her body.
    She travels slowly—her bowels are gone.
    She is dead on the shore
    & can travel no longer.
                    (Seri)

Or the singer/poet moves past empathy to take on the voice,
even the being, of the persons invoked:

    Imitate the spirit of the animal or thing inside you.
    Let the one who imitates the wolf, dance squatting. . .
    If he can, have him crack his knuckles & spurt blood.
                            (Lummi)

& again, the terror starting to edge in beside the comic mad-
ness:

    I thought I was a wolf
    but the owls are hooting
    & I'm afraid of the dark

    . . . .

    I am a wolf
    I go to many places
    I'm just tired of that one
                    (Sioux)

until the whole universe is alive: the rock in the Omaha sweathouse ritual ("listen / rock / old man / unmoving / living") or the stars ("we are the stars who sing") of the Passamaquoddy & those that animate the Ojibwa hunter:

> shining like a star—
> the animal that looks up's
> dazzled by my light

or earth again & again evoked:

> her hair became trees & grass
> her flesh the clay
> her bones the rocks
> her blood the springs of water
> (Thompson River)

into dizzying crescendos, voices of the thunder:

> with your moccasins of dark cloud, come to us
> with your mind enveloped in dark cloud, come to us
> with the dark thunder above you, come to us soaring
> with the shaped cloud at your feet, come to us soaring
> (Navajo)

& back to earth:

> Earth when it was made
> Sky when it was made
> Earth to the end
> Sky to the end
> (Apache)

Earth's people foremost, they find her or emerge from her & come, inevitably, to a single fixed point, "home," as center of their universe. This is the world described by Alfonso Ortiz for the Tewas of San Juan Pueblo: circles & peaks, & at the furthest mountains of the sacred earth (Conjilon Peak, Tsikomo, Sandia Crest, & Truchas Peak, none more than eighty miles away) the lake-dwelling, pre-emergent gods ("Dry Food Who Never Did Become"). The stages between the village & the places of the furthest gods are orderly (dance plazas, midden shrines, hills, & moutains), steps toward a greater & greater otherness, a wildness at the limits of the possibly human.

It was to the outskirts & past them that adventurers would go in hunt & vision quest, to contact allies in a search for "holiness," for "power," & for those ties that make a life "religious" (binding). In Black Elk's account, the quester went "crying for a vision" to a solitary mountaintop, where the people of the wilderness ("wingeds" & "four-leggeds," "even one as small & as seemingly insignificant as a little ant") came to him, as to the Eskimo shaman, for whom "all true wisdom is only to be learned far from the dwellings of men, out in the great solitudes." If the vision brought light—"bright, brighter even than the day" (Black Elk)—& beauty—"hills & fields & flowers & everything beautiful" (Essie Parrish)—it also brought darkness & terror:

> . . . the cries of the wind, the whisper of the trees, the voices of nature, animal sounds, the hooting of an owl. Suddenly I felt an overwhelming presence. Down there with me in my cramped hole was a big bird. . . . I could hear his cries, sometimes near and sometimes far, far away. I felt feathers or a wing touching my back and head. This feeling was so overwhelming that it was just too much for me. I trembled and my bones turned to ice. (Lame Deer)

The unknown, then, that thing that lives in wilderness (Cree *windigo* whose heart is ice), is also that which can destroy us.

Men seek these small deaths as if to arm themselves against the large one. In the Kwakiutls' Hamatsa ceremony, the initiates ventured beyond the boundaries of their coastal, river-hugging villages & engaged the beings of wilderness. There they were devoured by the truly wild one—"Cannibal at the North End of the World"—&, "born again," took on the wild one's "nature" (or let it arise within them), until the others brought them back, tamed them to live within the human. The enactments were extraordinary: a sense of ritual & theater ("transformances," Richard Schechner would call them) that could serve as models for present ventures (i.e., "the search for the primitive"—S. Diamond) in the same direction.

It is this willing & dangerous engagement, I would suggest, that informs in any instance the Indian approach to "wilderness." Earlier forms of life—animals, gods & proto-humans— appear to those (hunters & questers) who leave the "clearing" for the "forest." In the adventure of wilderness, the Indian hunter goes "primitive" & "native" (back to "nature"), with a sense of the primal, untamed past (where we came from, what we carry with us) as romantic as that of any neo-redskin of the 1960s/70s. A surviving Delaware foundation narrative, *The Walum Olum*, recalls the idealized primitives of the pre-Delaware past:

> in the beginning of the world
>   all men had knowledge cheerfully
>   all had leisure
>   all thoughts were pleasant
>
> at that time all creatures were friends. . . .

If the Delawares are in a "state of nature," they are also clearly looking backward to a "state of nature."

That backward look—that distancing from "wilderness"— can, in other situations, turn into a genuine despair. The more cultures expand—the more goods they place as obstacles between the human & non-human—the greater the split becomes. Somewhere, too, the walls begin to go up, & the civilized separation leads to a terror that's barely relieved; as in the generalized Aztec "definition" of *forest*, which rivals anything from Christian Europe in its equation of "wilderness" & "desert":

> There is no one; there are no people. It is desolate; it lies desolate. There is nothing edible. Misery abounds, misery emerges, misery spreads. There is no joy, no pleasure . . .

—until at a certain point (with "wilderness" far off), the terror shifts once more, appears in the settlement, the city itself, like Mesopotamian Gilgamesh, who looks over the walls of Uruk ("where man dies oppressed at heart"), sees "the bodies floating in the river," & sets his sights toward wilderness: "the country of the living." The same shifting contrast (good wilderness, bad wilderness, etc.) pervades Quetzalcoatl's flight from Tula to "the country of red daylight," or, in reverse, the return of the Huichol peyote hunters, who become their own ancestors on the journey to primal Wirikuta, but on the way back to the village sing:

Now I don't feel,
Now I don't feel,
Now I don't even feel like going to my rancho,
For there at my rancho it is so ugly,
And here in Wirikuta so green, so green . . .

—or the work of Simon Ortiz, contemporary poet from Acoma Pueblo, who finds, in the "new wilderness," the desert of Los Angeles, the threat of human loss without (for him) the voices of the older gods, drowned out by lifeless power:

I am under L. A. International Airport,
on the West Coast, someplace called America.
I am somewhat educated, I can read and use a compass;
yet the knowledge of where I am is useless.
Instead, it is a sad, disheartening burden.
I am a poor, tired wretch in this maze.
With its tunnels, its jet drones, its bland faces,
TV consoles, and its emotionless answers.
America has obliterated my sense of comprehension.
Without this comprehension, I am emptied
of any substance. America has finally caught me.
I meld into the walls of that tunnel
and become the silent burial. There are no echoes.

And this also is a part of the human experience we share.

New Wilderness Letter, Volume 2, Number 7, 1979.

THE POETICS OF SHAMANISM (1968)

The word "shaman" (Tungus: šaman) comes from Siberia & "in the strict sense is pre-eminently a religous phenomenon of Siberia & Central Asia" (Eliade). But the parallels elsewhere (North America, Indonesia, Oceania, China, etc.) are remarkable & lead also to a consideration of coincidences between "primitive-archaic" & modern thought. Eliade treats shamanism in-the-broader-sense as a specialized technique & ecstasy & the shaman as "technician-of-the-sacred." In this sense, too, the shaman can be seen as proto-poet, for almost always his technique hinges on the creation of special linguistic circumstances, i.e., of song & invocation.

In 1870 Rimbaud first used the term *voyant* (seer) to identify the new breed of poet who was to be "absolutely modern," etc.:

> one must, I say, become a seer,
>> make oneself into a seer

or, as Rasmussen writes of the Iglulik Eskimos:

> the young aspirant, when applying to a shaman, should always use the following formula
>> *takujumaqama*: I come to you
> because I desire to see

& the Copper Eskimos called the shaman-songman *"elik,* i.e., one who has eyes."'

●

In a typical (self)-initiation into shamanism, the new shaman experiences the breakdown of his familiar consciousness or world-view, and is led into a dream or vision at the center of which there is often a song or a series of songs "that force themselves out without any effort to compose them." [Thus: Isaac Tens, a Gitksan Indian practitioner cited in the accompanying text in *Technicians.*] The dream & vision aspect, in fact, goes way past any limits, however loosely drawn, of shamanism, into areas where a priesthood (as developer & transmitter of a *fixed* system) predominates, &, on the other hand, into areas where "all men" are "shamans," i.e., are "open" to the "gift" of vision & song. Thus:

The future (Bororo) shaman walks in the forest & suddenly sees a bird perch within reach of his hand, then vanish. Flocks of parrots fly down toward him & disappear as if by magic. The future shaman goes home shaking & uttering unintelligible words. An odor of decay . . . emanates from his body. Suddenly a gust of wind makes him totter; he falls like a dead man. At this moment he has become the receptacle of a spirit that speaks through his mouth. From now on he is a shaman. (A. Metraux, "Le Shamanisme chez les Indiens de l'Amérique du Sud tropicale," 1944, in Eliade, *Shamanism*, p. 82.)

He dreams of many things, & his body is muddled & becomes a house of dreams. And he dreams constantly of many things, & on awaking says to his friends: "My body is muddled today; I dreamt many men were killing me; I escaped I know not how. And on waking, one part of my body felt different from the other parts; it was no longer alike all over." (H. Callaway, *The Religious System of the Amazulu,* Natal, 1870, p. 259.)

All Blackfoot songs, except those learned from other tribes, are said to have been obtained through dreams or visions. . . . A man may be walking along & hear a bird, insect, stone or something else singing; he remembers the song & claims it as especially given to him. A man may get songs from a ghost in the same way. (C. Wissler, "Ceremonial Bundles of the Blackfoot Indians," *Anthropological Papers of the American Museum of Natural History,* Vol. VII, Part 2 [1912], p. 263.)

Anything, in fact, can deliver a song because anything— "night, mist, the blue sky, east, west, women, adolescent girls, men's hands & feet, the sexual organs of men & women, the bat, the land of souls, ghosts, graves, the bones, hair & teeth of the dead," etc.—is alive. (Thus: Wissler's listing.) Here is the central image of shamanism & of all "primitive" thought, the intuition (whether fiction or not doesn't yet matter) of a connected & fluid universe, as alive as a man is—just that much alive.

And all this seems thrust upon him—a unifying vision that brings with it the power of song & image, seen in his own terms as power to heal-the-soul & all disease viewed as disorder-of-the-soul, as disconnection & rigidity. Nor does he come to it easily—this apparent separation of himself from the normal orders of men—but often manifests what Eliade calls "a resistance to the divine election."

We're on familiar ground here, granted the very obvious differences in terminology & place, materials & techniques, etc. —recognizing in the shaman's experience that systematic derangement of the senses Rimbaud spoke of, not for its own sake but toward the possibility of sight & order. For the shaman-poet

> like the sick man . . . is projected onto a vital plane that shows him the fundamental data of human existence, that is, solitude, danger, hostility of the surrounding world. But the primitive magician, the medicine man, or the shaman is not only a sick man; he is, above all, a sick man who has been cured, who has succeeded in curing himself. (Eliade, *Shamanism*, p. 27.)

But the shaman's techniques-of-the-sacred made him, more than the modern poet, supreme physician & custodian of the soul. The belief was enough to validate the function—that he could climb to heaven or descend to the underworld or into the sea, could find a cure or an answer to misfortune, or after death guide the soul to its place-of-rest, etc.

In the rites accompanying a climb, a tree or ladder was generally used, but often too the shaman's drum was itself viewed as vehicle-of-motion; "the drum," said the Yakut shamans, "is our horse." The journey—to "heaven" or hell"—took place in stages marked by "obstacles," the shaman-songs being the keys to unlock them. Thus, when the Altaic "black" shaman in his descent reaches "the Chinese desert of red sand (&) rides over a yellow steppe that a magpie could not fly across, (he) cries to the audience: 'By the power of songs we cross it!' " In singing & dancing he has the help of assistants, & sometimes the audience joins him in chorus.

So, something more than literature is going on here: for ourselves, let me suggest, the question of how the concept & techniques of the "sacred" can persist in the "secular" world, not as nostalgia for the archaic past but (as Snyder writes) "a vehicle to ease us into the future."

Technicians of the Sacred.

GOD'S SEXUALITY (1968)

A heavy ripeness, the swelling & bursting of a teeming life-source, colors Australian views of the creation. The bandicoot-father, fullness of the new light, sweet dark juice of honeysuckle buds, a swarming sense of life—not two-by-two, in pairs, but *swarming*—was turned-from in the West, reduced to images of evil. Spenser's *Error* breeds "a thousand yong ones, which she dayly fed, / Sucking upon her poisonous dugs"; & Milton's *Sin* is the Prolific raped by her son into the production of "those yelling monsters, that with ceaseless cry / Surround me, as thou sawest, hourly conceived / And hourly born, with sorrow infinite," etc. But Blake renamed these "the Prolific" & marked a turning in man's relation to his "sensual existence."

God's sexuality—lonely, hermaphroditic—is thus another, very natural way of imagining the creation. The most famous such account in the ancient Near East was the Egyptian masturbation genesis:

> Heaven had not been created . . .
> The earth had not been created . . .
> I formed a spell in my heart . . .
> I made forms of every kind . . .
> I thrust my cock into my closed hand . . .
> I made my seed to enter my hand . . .
> I poured it into my mouth . . .
> I broke wind under the form of SHU . . .
> I passed water under the form of TEFNUT . . .

But even the priestly Genesis (Hebrew) couldn't unhook the mind from its old imaginings, hypotheses, etc.; *vide* the section collaged into the beginning of the fifth chapter:

> This is the book of the generations of Adam. In the day
>   that God created man, *in the likeness of God* made
>   he *him*;

> *Male & female* created he them; & blest them, & *called*
> *their name Adam.*

But the idea—re-explored in the medieval *Zohar*—was already
very old.

Technicians of the Sacred.

AMERICA AS A WOMAN (1973)

In *In the American Grain,* William Carlos Williams writes:
"One is forced on the conception of the New World as a
woman." In that form he has her speaking to De Soto, he who
would soon be buried in her waters, "this solitary sperm . . .
into the liquid, the formless, the insatiable belly of sleep;
down among the fishes." She had told him while alive to

> . . . ride upon the belly of the waters, building your boats
> to carry all across. Calculate for the current; the boats move
> with a force not their own, up and down, sliding upon that
> female who communicates to them, across all else, herself.
> And still there is that which you have not sounded, under
> the boats, under the adventure—giving to all things the
> current, the wave, the onwash of my passion. So cross and
> have done with it you are safe—and I am desolate. . . .
> Follow me—if you can. Follow me, Señor, this is your
> country. I give it to you. Take it.

We have encountered that woman-thing before—a nearly uni-
versal myth of "Mother Earth," or of the land, that which we
wrench from Earth, with pleasure at first, then in a dream of
losses endlessly repeated. She is Blake's Jerusalem (*and*
Oothoon-Enitharmon): the one the Jews called the Shekinah;
the Gnostics called Sophia; the Tantrists called Goddess-of-
Wisdom-Whose-Substance-Is-Desire and in her terrifying as-
pect, Kali. The Indian nations knew her too, as the mother
sometimes or grandmother, sometimes as the woman on a jour-
ney, like the one for whom the mound in Upper Michigan was
called Where-she-with-the-full-belly-turned-over.

In the story of American poetry she turns up often. She is
earth or god, wisdom or muse—or that woman always one
town ahead of our pursuit, say, or like the poor-old-soul of
Bukka White's blues, singing.

I ain't got nobody
To take me to this train
Mmmmmmmmmmmmmmmmmmmmmmmmmmmmmmmmmmmmmm
Mmmmmmmmmmmm mmmm mm mm mm

as real in her desolation as America in hers. Wrote Edgar
Allen Poe, "The death, then, of a beautiful woman is, un-
questionably, the most poetical topic in the world."

America a Prophecy, with George Quasha.

OFFERING FLOWERS (1968)

> *I offer flowers. I sow flower seeds. I plant flowers. I assemble*
> *flowers. I pick flowers. I pick different flowers. I remove flow-*
> *ers. I seek flowers. I offer flowers. I arrange flowers.*
> —BERNARDINO DE SAHAGÚN, *Florentine Codex*:
> *A General History of the Things of*
> *New Spain*

The Aztecs (they say) rode on lakes of flowers, & decorated bodies, gods & houses with flowers, which their language made into synonyms for speech/heart/soul & for the sun as world-heart/world-flower. Men waged a "flowering war" of the spirit in which "if spirit wins," writes Laurette Sejourné, "the body 'flowers' & a new light goes to give power to the Sun." Only later, the Aztec rulers literalized this into a series of staged battles against already conquered peoples, that the foredoomed losers paid for (literally) with their hearts. So, too, the ninth-month ceremony called The Flowers Are Offered (the only monthly ritual without human sacrifice) was not devoted to Xochipilli, the god of flowers & the soul, but to the war god Huitzilopochtli.

Correspondences of heart & word & flower are repeated by the Japanese Seami, who speaks of the "flower" (the "flower-thought" of the Buddhists) as the Nō actor's hidden ability, a matter of the heart & voice. In the dance & gesture language of India, Wilson D. Wallis tells us,

> when the fingers are straight & are brought together so that the tips touch, the gesture means "flower bud." When con-veyed to the mouth & thrust outward, it means "speech." In Hawaii this gesture means "flower"; or, if made at the mouth, it means "talk" or "song." (In Stanley Diamond, ed., *Culture in History: Essays in Honor of Paul Radin*.)

But it's the same too in Francis of Assisi's "little flowers" & in the dead words of our own language that speak of eloquence as "flowery" or "florid"—terms that have lost their currency, except when Carlos Williams, say, makes them alive again in "*Asphodel, That Greeny Flower.*" And there are other instances to remind us, & a memory perhaps of that "great flower" of Dante's—"high fantasy" he called it, & "living flame."

Technicians of the Sacred.

TREE SPIRIT EVENTS (1978)

Then sing the trees of the wood for joy
before the Lord.

One mounts to one side.
One descends on that side.
One enters between the two.
Two crown themselves with a third.
Three enter into one.
One produces various colors.
Six of them descend on one side & six of them on the other.
Six enter into twelve.
Twelve bestir themselves to form twenty-two.
Six are comprised in ten.
Ten are fixed in one.

(*Zohar*)

COMMENTARY: ". . . He had studied all manners of speech /
even the utterances of mountains, hills & valleys / the utter-
ance of trees & plants / the utterance of beasts & animals / He
had learned them all"; thus an early description of Hillel the
Elder (first centuries B.C./A.D.), showing that reintegration
with the natural world that characterizes the subterranean side
of the Western mystical tradition. But the obvious animism
of the medieval "tree events" here given—identification of the
trees of Eden with angels, etc.—combines as well with the
numerology of Jewish mysticism & *poesis*. [See above, page
156.] Also, since numbers & letters are here identical, the
reader (if acquainted with such works as Graves's *The White
Goddess*) may recognize a resemblance to Celtic tree alphabets,
etc.

A Big Jewish Book.

GIFT EVENT (1968, 1972)

Kwakiutl

Start by giving away different colored glass bowls.
Have everyone give everyone else a glass bowl.
Give away handkerchiefs & soap & things like that.
Give away a sack of clams & a roll of toilet paper.
Give away teddybear candies, apples, suckers & oranges.
Give away pigs & geese & chickens, or pretend to do so.
Pretend to be different things.
Have the women pretend to be crows, have the men pretend
to be something else.
Talk Chinese or something.
Make a narrow place at the entrance of a house & put a line
at the end of it that you have to stoop under to get in.
Hang the line with all sorts of pots & pans to make a big
noise.
Give away frying pans while saying things like "Here is this
frying pan worth $100 & this one worth $200."
Give everyone a new name.
Give a name to a grandchild or think of something & go &
get everything.

COMMENTARY: Compare Alison Knowles' *Giveaway Construction* (1963):

> Find something you like in the street & give it away. Or find
> a variety of things, make something of them, & give it
> away . . .

among many contemporary happenings, etc. that involve gift-
giving. Part of the redistribution pattern for valued objects,
or way of creating new value, but no more sinister (as pot-
latch or as art) here than there.

Shaking the Pumpkin.

THE GHOST DANCE (1968)

The late nineteenth-century messianic movement called the Ghost Dance was not simply a pathetic reaction to White rule or confused attempt to suck-up Christian wisdom. The ritual use of ecstasy & the dance is clearly more Indian than Christian; & the movement's central belief that the present world would go the way of all previous worlds through destruction & re-emergence had been (for all the Christian turns it was now given) widespread throughout North America and at the heart, say, of the highly developed religious systems of the Mexican plateau.

The "messiah" of the Ghost Dance was Wovoka ("the cutter"), also called Jack Wilson, who *circa* 1889 was taken up to heaven by God & there given the message of redemption, with full control over the elements, etc. His doctrine spread quickly through the Indian world, under various names but always referring to the trance-like dance at its center; thus "dance in a circle" (Paiute), "everybody dragging" (Shoshoni), "the Fathers' dance" (Comanche), "dance with clasped hands" & "dance craziness" (Kiowa), & "ghost dance" (Sioux & Arapaho). Wovoka's own dance was described by a northern Cheyenne follower named Porcupine in terms reminiscent of Jesus' "round dance" with his disciples in the apocryphal & equally "unchristian" Acts of St. John:

> They cleared off a space in the form of a circus ring & we all gathered there . . . The Christ [i.e., Wovoka] was with them . . . I looked around to find him, & finally saw him sitting on one side of the ring. . . . They made a big fire to throw light on him . . . He sat there a long time & nobody went up to speak to him. He sat with his head bowed all the time. After a while he rose & said he was very glad to see his children. . . . "My children, I want you to listen to all I have to say to you. I will teach you, too, how to dance a dance, & I want you to dance it. Get ready for your dance & then, when the dance is over, I will talk to you."

He was dressed in a white coat with stripes. The rest of his dress was a white man's except that he had on a pair of moccasins. Then he commenced our dance, everybody joining in, the Christ singing while we danced. . . . (Later) he commenced to tremble all over, violently for a while, & then sat down. We danced all that night, the Christ lying down beside us apparently dead.

Of the songs themselves James Mooney who gathered them writes: "All the songs are adapted to the simple measure of the dance step . . . the dancers moving from right to left, following the course of the sun . . . hardly lifting the feet from the ground. . . . Each song is started in the same manner, first in an undertone while singers stand still in their places, & then with full voice as they begin to circle around. At intervals between the songs . . . the dancers unclasp hands & sit down to smoke or talk for a few minutes. . . . There is no limit to the number of these songs, as every trance at every dance produces a new one. . . . Thus a single dance may easily result in twenty or thirty new songs."

This intense existence at the level of poetry was an abiding characteristic of those nations of poets who were defeated or driven onto reserves by armies of European businessmen & farmers. But, writes Gary Snyder: "The American Indian is the vengeful ghost lurking in the back of the troubled American mind. Which is why we lash out with such ferocity & passion, so muddied a heart, at the black-haired young peasants & soldiers who are the 'Viet Cong.' That ghost will claim the next generation as its own. When this has happened, citizens of the USA will at last begin to be Americans, truly at home on the continent, in love with their land. The chorus of a Cheyenne Indian Ghost Dance song: "hiniswa'vita'ki'ni—'we shall live again.' "

And even so, the pronoun of the song—the "we"—still seems elusive: the Indians refuse to be mere "ghosts," while the realities of language & of culture, built over centuries, remain the hardest to hold on to or to claim as something new.

Technicians of the Sacred.

199

JESUS (1978)

The figure of Jesus emerges, dark & shining in the pattern of other Jewish messiahs from then to present, & enters history. With him he carries the older metaphors of transformation: *I will make you a god to Pharaoh . . . the Patriarchs are the Merkaba . . . Israel the first born, logos . . . son of God*— working the change not only on himself but on his fellow Jews as well. For it is from this point that *we* are drawn into the paranoia of the *other:* are transformed ("betrayers," "murderers") & locked into a system of thought, of action & response, which dominates & robs us of control over our lives.

The Jews, by Jesus' time, had already moved into the world outside Judaea. With the wars of that first century the land itself was taken from them—irrevocably in the Christian triumph that would follow. The visible Jewish response was further to literalize the Torah, to bring all into the domain of the written: to replace the broken temple with the study house, the rites of sacrifice with those of prayers & exegesis. But beneath that surface other forces stirred: a secret transmission or kabbala that kept alive a poetics of liberation & an anger that produced further messiahs, further failed revolutionaries & mystics, fantasies of escape from exile, & a continuing dream of freedom in a world in which "a fence was built around the Law."

For the later messiahs Jesus remained a covert model. Multiphasic from the start, he appeared in a variety of forms to the early Jewish Christians, including the dancer-of-the-mysteries & playful trickster in the gnostic Acts of St. John. Thus he was himself a creature of the *nous poetikos* (creative mind) that would proliferate his image through the world. But the source of that image was still Jewish: prophetic & visionary & sharing that other side of the Jewish psyche that Gershom Scholem describes for Sabbatai Zevi, messiah of a later age: "[a movement] with its doctrine so profoundly shocking to the Jewish conception of things that the violation of the Torah could become its true fulfillment . . . [yet] a dialectical outgrowth of the belief in [his] Messiahship. . . . Not only . . . a single continuous development which retained its identity in the eyes of its adherents regardless of whether they themselves remained Jews or not, but also, paradoxical though it may seem, a specifically *Jewish* phenomenon. . . ." (From *The Messianic Idea in Judaism*)

A Big Jewish Book.

THE NIGHT CHANT (1968)

With the dark thunder above you, come to us soaring
With the shapen cloud at your feet, come to us soaring
With the far darkness made of the dark cloud over your head,
    come to us soaring
With the far darkness made of the rain & mist over your head,
    come to us soaring

—From *The Navajo Night Chant,*
tr. Washington Matthews (1902)

Night Chant or Night Way is only one part of the very complex Navajo system of myths & ceremonies directed mainly toward healing. Other chants or ways include the monumental Beauty Way & Blessing Way, as well as Mountain Way, Flint Way, Enemy Way, Prostitution Way, Life Way, Shooting Way, Red Ant Way, Monster Way, Moving Up Way, etc.—each with special functions, each consisting of many songs, events, & myths-of-origin—with multiple subdivisions and reconstructions thereof. The whole chantway system is so complicated in fact that the individual priest or chanter (*hatali,* literally, a keeper-of-the-songs) can rarely keep-in-mind more than a single ceremony like the nine-day Night Chant, sometimes only part of one. There's also more room for variation by the individual singer than at first meets-the-eye—& this is itself a part of the system since, in transmitting the ceremonies, a gap is invariably left that the new singer must fill-in on his own.

As with other "primitive" art of this complexity, the Night Chant is very much "intermedia," though on the ninth night (from which this excerpt is taken) the singing dominates & is "uninterrupted . . . from dark until daylight." At the start of this song, writes Matthews:

> patient & shaman [have positions] in the west, facing the
> east, & the priest prays a long prayer to each god, which the

patient repeats after him, sentence by sentence. . . . The four prayers are alike in all respects, except in the mention of certain attributes of the gods. . . . [The one given here is addressed] to the dark bird who is the chief of [the sacred] pollen. While [it] is being said, the dancer keeps up a constant motion, bending & straightening the left knee, & swaying the head from side to side.

While the complexity of Night Chant, etc., necessitates a collective effort in performance & transmission, the legend of its founding credits the inspiration to Bitahatini, literally His-Imagination, His-Visions, but freely translated as The Visionary. Carried off by the gods he brought back the rites for this chant (of sandpainting, dance & masks, etc.) along with the songs & instructions for curing. The Navajos said of him:

Whenever he went out by himself, he heard the songs of spirits sung to him, or thought he heard them sung. . . . His three brothers had no faith in him. They said: "When you have returned from your solitary walks & tell us you have seen strange things & heard strange songs, you are mistaken, you only imagine you hear these songs & you see nothing unusual." Whenever he returned from one of these lonely rambles he tried to teach his brothers the songs he had heard; but they would not listen to him.

The reader may want to compare this early experience of The Visionary's with that of Isaac Tens* & the nature of his spirit-journey with Black Elk's "Great Vision" (Lakota) recorded in John Neihardt's *Black Elk Speaks*. While these accounts are from three Indian groups that are supposed to be far apart in their approaches to the sacred, the experiences show a common (shamanic/not priestly) pattern, with echoes throughout the "primitive & archaic" worlds. Neruda's vision of his dead friend Jimenez, with its presumably coincidental

* Gitksan Indian shaman mentioned in the piece on shamanism, above. Hunting in the wilderness, he was beseiged by "huge birds & other animals," fell into a trance, & in that visionary state received the sacred songs he used in curing.

use of a Night Chant refrain (*vienes volando* = come flying, or come soaring), opens still further areas for speculation:

Amid frightening feathers, nights,
amid magnolias, amid telegrams,
with the south and west sea winds
    you come flying.

Under tombs, under ashes,
under frozen snails,
under the earth's deepest waters
    you come flying.

And deeper, between drowned children,
blind plants and rotting fish,
out through the clouds again
    you come flying.

More distant than blood and bone,
more distant than bread, than wine,
more distant than fire
    you come flying . . .

Etcetera

—From Clayton Eshleman's translation of
   Alberto Rojas Jimenez Viene Volando

Technicians of the Sacred.

KUNAPIPI (1968)

Kunapipi is the name of a major Australian fertility cult, which centers on "a Great Mother, expressed as either a single or dual personality, her power being extended to her daughters, the Wauwalak." In the myth, these (two) Wauwalak Sisters leave their home territory after the elder has incestuous relations with a clansman & becomes pregnant. At a sacred water hole she gives birth to a child, blood from the afterbirth attracting a great python (Julunggul), who lives in the hole. Then, writes R. M. Berndt in *Kunapipi: A Study of an Australian Aboriginal Religious Cult*:

> . . . the sky was shut in with clouds: a storm broke, summoned by Julunggul. They washed the baby, to get rid of the smell of blood, but it was too late. Night had fallen. They crouched in the hut by the fire while the rain poured down outside, taking it in turns to dance and to call ritually in an effort to drive away the storm. When the elder sister danced . . . the rain dwindled to almost nothing. When the younger sister did this, she could check the storm only a little. Then they sang Kunapipi songs, and the storm died down.

Later the Sisters are swallowed & vomited up—thus the ancient pattern of death & resurrection, etc.

But the relation of myth to ritual-event & song is complicated far beyond the simple telling. The ceremonial ground is at once the place-of-the-snake & womb-of-the-mother; & the myth is always a real presence behind the Kunapipi songs, forming (on other ceremonial occasions) the basis of both sacred & secular cycles with a clearly "narrative" quality. Here it's (mostly) present through allusion, the songs' actual "content" consisting of descriptions of accompanying ceremonial activities, particularly of ritual intercourse between clansmen (fertility "magic" sanctioned by the elder sister's incest) & of "fire-throwing" (djamala) that "symbolizes the lightning sent by Julunggul." Bullroarers of cypress bark reproduce the python's roaring in the storm; also, the songs & dances are said to be those of the mythic beings themselves—the Sisters dancing to postpone the coming of the snake, etc.

Of the songs *per se* Berndt writes: "Like the majority of songs in Aboriginal Australia, these consist of 'key' words, which seem to us to need further explanation, but are usually understood by natives singing or participating in the ritual. These 'key' words, several of which constitute a song, are really word pictures. . . . In short songs of this type in particular, the meaning of a word usually depends entirely upon the context. . . . Moreover . . . a song that is sung in one context, to a specific part of the rituals, may have one meaning, while in another context it has a different meaning." There are also different classes of words with the same "meaning": some open to the whole community, some requiring special knowledge, some used only in singing, etc. A typical run of songs follows:

1	"penis"	incisure	incisure
	penis	penis	semen

2   Semen white like the mist

3   with penis erect
the kangaroo
moves its buttocks

4   step by step
(she) walks away from coitus
her back to them

5   the catfish swimming
& singing

6   the bullroarer's string

7   The nipples of the young girl's breasts protrude—
& the musk of her vagina—

8   creek
moving
"creek"

9   mist covering
       the river

10   cypress branches
       cypress cone
       seeds of the cone

The relation to contemporary practice—structure & image—
seems inescapable.

Technicians of the Sacred.

THE RAINGOD DRAMA (1972)

The Raingod Drama (Nu·hi) is a yearly celebration performed by the Winter Moiety at San Juan Pueblo in New Mexico. Its culmination is an evening/night in which the Kachinas (raingods) appear in a performance heralded & led by two clowns of the kind called *kosa* (Hopi: *paiyakyamu*; Zuni: *koshari*). The "goddess" addressed therein is the one through whom the Winter Cacique (= religious leader of the Winter Moiety) receives his strength; sometimes in fact the Cacique himself is called O·yi·ka, the root meaning of which is "ice." Neither the Cacique nor any of the people present are an audience for the dramatic event, but all are active participants: something that distinguishes theater as ritual from theater as spectator sport.

The comic as religious form is central to tribal practice & reminds us that laughter may have been the first religious language, that it may in fact be latent in much religious experience as we know it or overt among those contemporaries of ours who are still tribal or living closer to their tribal roots. The "sacred clowns" (as Alfonso Ortiz calls them—in their role of "an anti-priest who presides over the anti-rites") keep man down-to-earth while acting as intermediaries for powers that reach beyond (if not above) the human. So do the masked dancers (the Kachinas of the present work), but with the balance tilted toward the more-than-human, whose language we don't understand & don't dare laugh at. Both reflect the ambiguity of the sacred (dream)-life as it incredibly attempts to reach us, charged as it is with the danger of something that goes against our (waking) sense of how-things-are. But in the spirit world (they sometimes tell us) everything appears reversed, as it does too in the speech & actions of the Clowns, in the incomprehensible "language" of the Kachinas, in the silence of the last Kachina of the Raingod Drama, who is also the old man doing the thing that young men do best, etc. In response to this, the laughter that fills the people's throats & is itself convulsive & uncontrollable may be felt as a force speaking through man: the language of the gods deflected in the medium of our human world. (A language too that poets in our own time may again be learning to speak!)

The pivot of the god-comedy, as it reveals itself in these terms, is the Man Ceremony. After the other Kachinas leave, a last one, silent & plain in appearance, enters & takes part in a mock "marriage" with a young virgin. The silent one acts as the contrary of the other raingods, going from their grunts & whistles to his own total silence, but playing that too against the relentlessness of his stalking, which is both that of the hunter & the fiercely sexed old man. The translator of the Raingod Drama, Vera Laski, gives a description of its full (if "non-musical") exploitation of sound, which links it too with many discoveries & rediscoveries in contemporary music, etc. Unlike other Pueblo rituals it uses neither singing, drums, nor rattles, but a range of other sounds & "noises" to convey a sense of the Kachinas as a force of nature: stomping feet (for thunder), bullroarers (for the "roaring wind"), turtle shells tied to the Clowns' moccasins, bells (or bits of deerhoofs or pig knuckles) around the Raingods' waists & ankles. In addition—& this, writes Laski, is the most imporant bit of all—"each Raingod has his own particular vocal sounds that identify him . . . voices that utter weird sounds which belong to no human language . . ." rather to "the language of the gods." And against these "many weird sounds, deep & shrill, resounding & piercing," the silence of the final Kachina & the silence that surrounds his entrance must be included—part of an ongoing modulation of sound that represents a high conception of the boundaries of noise & silence.

The San Juan name for the Silent One is either *Yeŋ sedó* = Old Man or *Povi yeŋ* = Flower Man, & his name in turn becomes a joking term for penis, just as Man Ceremony itself may be a synonym for fucking—at least where unexpected or especially exciting. Ambiguous enough all by himself the old man is further set against the young virgin, like two extremes of nature brought together, as opposites are always joined in that fusion from which the sacred comes to life in poem or other such implosion. This "uniting of opposites" is for the Pueblos (Laski writes) "a symbol of harmony," just as sex is in general. Says the formula of the Initiation Ceremony: "Be a man & be a woman," & the words are repeated in other aspects of Pueblo life, wherever the supernatural intervenes.

Shaking the Pumpkin.

RAIN EVENT ONE (1978)

Whisper until it rains.

COMMENTARY:
(1)   The Hebrew word for magic—"kishuf"—literally "murmuring" or "muttering."

(2)   "If you see a generation over whom the heavens are rust-colored like copper so that neither rain nor dew falls, it is because that generation is wanting in whisperers. What then is the remedy? Let them go to someone who knows how to whisper." (Talmud B. *Ta'an* 8a)

(3)   "In oriental countries in general, the Jews have acquired for one reason or another, a special reputation as rainmakers." (Raphael Patai, *The Hebrew Goddess*)

A Big Jewish Book.

OLD MAN COYOTE (1972)

Coyote appears throughout the Americas in the familiar role of primordial shit-thrower, cock-erupter, etc., to satisfy the need for all that in the full pantheon of essential beings:

> . . . and Coon said Not that way! What I do, I put my prick into a nest of ants, they bite it, maybe hard, and there's a big fried fish, a little bite, I get a small fish. Well Coyote did it, he found the ants & put his prick in them, it really hurt when they bit; Coyote thought about his fish and pulled out his prick all red and sore. Home with no fish Coyote said to Coon They bit my thing and hurt it but I got no fish
>
> (Armand Schwerner's version from the Nez Percé)

No merely horny version of a Disney character, he is (like other tricksters in tribal America: Rabbit, Raven, Spider, Bluejay, Mink, Flint, Glooscap, Saynday, etc.) the product of a profound & comic imagination playing upon the realities of man & nature. Thus, as Jung writes of the Winnebagos' Trickster in that now-famous essay: he is "absolutely undifferentiated human consciousness . . . a psyche that has hardly left the animal level . . . (but) god, man and animal at once . . . both sub- and super-human . . . an expression (therefore) of the polaristic nature of the psyche, which like any other energic system is dependent on the tension of opposites." Like any genuine poetry system too.

Among the Crow, as in other Indian religions, he appears as the Supreme Trickster but also as the first maker of the earth & all living things. "He was a great trickster & our ruler," says another narrator. "And since he was a great trickster, we are that way also." But he adds: "All the ways of the Indians he made for us. He put us to sleep, he made us dream, whatever he wanted us to do we did. He put the stars into this world in the beginning; they were dangerous." (Robert H. Lowie, *Religion of the Crow*)

The good-of-him, which should be more apparent than ever to "counter-culturists," etc. (he is the favored "god" for sure of a generation or two of New American Poets), is at least three-fold:

(1) to find a place for what—as animals, children, etc.—we were & are: to be aware of, even to enjoy, the very thing that scares us with threats of madness, loss of self, etc.;

(2) to ridicule our ordinary behaviors by breaking (vicariously at least) their hold on us: to punch holes in established authority (= the way things are) so as not to be its forever silent victims;

(3) where Trickster is creator too, to explain the dangers inherent in reality itself—of a world, that is, that must have such gods at its inception: or as old Ten'a Indian said to John Chapman, "The Creator made all things good, but the Raven (= Trickster) introduced confusion": & the Nez Percé, while giving him a still more terrifying edge: *"with blood-stained mouth / comes mad Coyote!"*

Thus Old Man Coyote is the imperfect (= dangerous) creator of an imperfect (= dangerous) universe—a view which, being more empirical & rational in the first place, presents fewer problems to rationalize than the Christian view, say, of a perfect god & universe, etc. "Existential man. Dostoyevsky coyote." (S. Ortiz)

Shaking the Pumpkin, passim.

CRAZY DOG EVENTS (1972)

Crow

1.   Act like a crazy dog. Wear sashes & other fine clothes, carry
a rattle, & dance along the roads singing crazy dog songs after
everyone else has gone to bed.

2.   Talk crosswise: say the opposite of what you mean & make
others say the opposite of what they mean in return.

3.   Fight like a fool by rushing up to an enemy & offering to
be killed. Dig a hole near an enemy, & when the enemy sur-
rounds it, leap out at them & drive them back.

4.   Paint yourself white, mount a white horse, cover its eyes
& make it jump down a steep & rocky bank, until both of you
are crushed.

COMMENTARY: The events resemble Dada activities, say, but
also the political gestures of the provos & crazies, etc. of the
late 1960s. But the phenomenon (part of tribal American
sacred clown traditions) was a deep-seated aspect of Plains
Indian warrior life, not unlike traditional patterns of the
Japanese & others. In that sense it both supported a culture
& challenged its rigidities.

In a narrative by Yellow-brow, a young warrior named
Double-face, enduring the typical *ennui* of a Crazy Dog mem-
ber pledged to self-destructive madness, wanders feverishly
around camp the day before battle with the Cheyenne. He
says to his older brother: "There are three things I am now
eager to do: I want to sing a sacred song; I want to sing a Big
Dog song; I want to cry." Then he paints his horse & himself,
fits on medicines, & goes into the camp circle, crying & making
others cry, wailing a prayer.

Actions of the Crazy Dog Society (but literally Crazy-Dog-
wishing-to-die) were extreme & futile but heroic too: a very

literal playing-out of older Plains Indian despair over death & old age—a kind of behavior not that foreign to our own lives lived at extremes, etc. "Why have you done that?" Spotted-rabbit's mother asked. "You are one of the best-situated young men . . . you are one of the most fortunate men who ever lived . . . & were always happy." But, writes Robert Lowie, Spotted-rabbit was bored with life because he could not get over his father's death. Or again, when Spotted-rabbit receives a gift of plums, he says, "I began to be a Crazy Dog early in the spring & did not think I should live so long; yet here I am today eating plums." Comments Lowie of such as Double-face & Spotted-rabbit: "We have here reached the peak of the Crow spirit."

Shaking the Pumpkin, passim.

5 / Thwarting Ends: A Post-Face

The only absolutes for poetry are diversity & change (& the freedom to pursue these); & the only purpose, over the long run, is to raise questions, to raise doubts, to put people into alternative, sometimes uncomfortable situations, to raise questions but not necessarily answer them, or to jump ahead with other questions, to challenge the most widely held of preconceptions in our culture, that "Western man" is the culmination of the human evolutionary process.

THE THWARTING OF ENDS:
AN INTERVIEW (1979)

INTERVIEWER: You are best known for your work in setting out a series of connections between contemporary poetry and art and a very wide range of traditional poetries, particularly those which haven't been accepted in the traditional Western framework. In what way is this work a reflection of the times?

ROTHENBERG: It is a reflection of some real part of the culture in search of meaningfulness, which is not necessarily the complete American picture. The situation we're all confronted by, that of a world that's been reduced to an increasingly lifeless shell, obviously creates great discomfort and anxiety. Therefore, a yearning for something else and a search for how it may have existed elsewhere. Most artists I know are involved with both of these but mainly as a personal search and less in reaching out to other times and places.

INTERVIEWER: A major part of your energy, however, seems to have gone into working with the past. Why?

ROTHENBERG: It's a passion. The whole thing—the transformation of life within the shell—is nailed down, cemented in my mind at least, when it doesn't affect only the present but our whole sense of time and place, of history and culture. Changes in the present are significant if they also change the concept of the past.

INTERVIEWER: What is this "transformation?"

ROTHENBERG: In general the impulse of serious modern art has been toward transformation, the idea that transformation and change itself are fundamental to human life: to welcome change rather than be terrified by it, to open up to the possibility of being able to live with contradictions, because truth, reality, isn't static, but like the mind, in a process of changing. I tend to back away from dogmatic assertions about how the world is and therefore how it must be, simply because of the evidence of historical harm that has been done by positions of that sort.

So what tends to interest me in traditional and tribal cultures is not that they maintain a status quo, but the way in which change is built into the relatively harmonious, communalistic, egalitarian framework of these usually very small cultures, and how their art and poetry function to allow change and transformation and to foster the sense of a living universe.

What we've lost is that sense of a living universe and the interconnection of all living beings. This was handled very badly by Western religions, was kept going by some poets and mystics, and began to be recovered definitively in the nineteenth-century scientific framework, in the Darwinian theory of evolution. I find myself not hostile to that aspect of science— making animals ancestors . . . restoring us as biological beings.

INTERVIEWER: To which aspects of science are you hostile?

ROTHENBERG: Not to science (= knowing) but to that other, increasing dependence on a technology which takes us away from the source of our own independent powers and which is coming to a critical phase now. The dependency of the individual on distant sources of power, which the energy crisis itself brings into question.

INTERVIEWER: How would you restructure society?

ROTHENBERG: All that I would propose under the circumstances is to develop again a kind of particular and local consciousness, a diversity and a self-sufficiency as far as that's possible and as far as it's meaningful. I wouldn't adopt a totally anti-technological stance unless it becomes necessary, and I wouldn't favor any localism that denies others the right to their own diversity.

INTERVIEWER: What tribal elements would you infuse into modern society?

ROTHENBERG: The sense of significance and meaning both deep and up close to the surface, permeating every aspect of work, so work itself is not divided from play. In the tribes there has been a communal creation of an imagined but not necessarily unreal world, a creation over tremendously long periods of time; and this long work (like the evolutionary work of species formation) in a certain sense can't be duplicated. What certain artists have done is to create descriptions of a meaningful world within their own lives and works—in contrast to American Indian culture, say, which consists of hundreds of smaller cultures, cultural patterns, languages, religions, mythologies developed as a result of thousands of years of human history. At the same time that we're depleting the store of fossil fuel, we've been depleting the number of existing animal species and the world's independent and semi-independent cultures. Those real cultures become less and less a resource humanity can draw from, but their extinction as such seems to draw less attention or concern than the other extinctions.

INTERVIEWER: So where does this leave modern man?

ROTHENBERG: It throws us back on our own resources and on a memory of what traditional cultures have been. My passion is to maintain and shore up what comes to us as a larger human memory, and to preserve as far as possible—and not in a museum sense—the real, continuous and localized cultures, the diversity that still exists in the world: to thwart by all means the other process toward a homogenization of cultures into a single monoculture.

There's a problem of creativity becoming unlocalized and broadcast from a few dominant central points until we're all hooked into the great communications network which tends to make our music and our art for us. In terms of the monoculture, our way of looking at ourselves in the world is conditioned for us from a greater and greater distance. And the worst thing about it is we don't know it's happening. We get to like it and think it's a creation we share—like commercial Rock, and so on.

INTERVIEWER: What waters your roots in this kind of society?

ROTHENBERG: A certain amount of creative work: writing, performing, singing. And the work and enthusiasm of many others, artists and ordinary people, who still assert a difference. But I'm realistic enough to see our limits and our fortune. We are still living in privileged circumstances in a country that continues to have a surplus of wealth and energy while other parts of the world live in horrendous conditions of poverty. Even with the cost of oil going up, it's still a country with energy to burn. That doesn't mean we don't have deep poverty, but we still operate off the leavings. The question is, How long can this be maintained? We may be at the latter end of a very brief period in human history. We continue to hold out the hope of alternative sources of energy which may or may not be developed, but in the last ten years we've come out of that "energy high." Maybe solar energy will be developed, or nuclear energy won't be destructive, but maybe not. It's this "maybe not," which has come up for us. There were so many of us who grew up with the sense that it would all go upward and onward. So, maybe not this generation, but another may be confronted by the question of maintaining itself in something resembling a total human life under vastly limited circumstances. We may, like other people, be forced back on our own resources, if it all doesn't result in utter catastrophe. At what point do people give up their cars? At five dollars a gallon? And which ones give it up? When does it come back to roost, to prove to us that America is at the service of the very rich . . . the avaricious? When will the disproportion between America and the outside world be translated into a worse disproportion at home? Speaking realistically, the last decade seems to have put us further away from a solution.

INTERVIEWER: If you won't offer a solution to these problems, what will you offer?

ROTHENBERG: What I can put my hands on: some mappings of the multiple ways in which human beings have dealt with their physical, spiritual and artistic lives, in the hopes that somebody may be able to use these maps, and also with the fear those maps may be used selfishly and with little idea of the common good. What worries me is the misuse of art and ritual in the context of a powerful and organized political structure.

INTERVIEWER: It has been said that you deliberately pursue certain aspects of mysticism in your anthologies. Is this true?

ROTHENBERG: I look for those points where mystical activity and poetic activity appear similar. I have a sense that poetry is not simply what is called "poetry," which usually refers to a semi-professional literary activity. I think poetry is involved with the creation of meaning through language. There are a lot of boundaries which get crossed here. Poetry is attempting to discover the otherwise unknowable. Science won't deal with the unknowable, it's the mystic and poet who do. In the highest meaning of the words, they have the *chutzpah* or *hubris* to do this. Poets are not necessarily modest in what they set out to do, nor are mystics. I'm amused by this. I think it's absolutely wonderful and crazy that people should try to know the unknowable. (Not the unknown, by the way, which is a very different matter.) I think what happens is that you get a lot of contradictory propositions . . . and that helps to thwart the monoculture and the single-minded total state. At the same time, my own approach is increasingly comic.

INTERVIEWER: What ideas, specifically, does your poetry challenge?

ROTHENBERG: At its simplest, the widespread idea that a poem is conventionally definable as such: that it rhymes, has a certain number of fixed rhythmical units per line, that a series of conventional forms developed from fourteenth through sixteenth-century Europe represents the culmination of poetic form. Another area open to challenge was the notion of poetry as elegance of expression, not newness of thought: what Pope said "was often thought but n'er so well expressed." From the idea of the conventional poem I would extend the challenge to the idea of the conventional person or the conventional society, and so on.

I think the challenge of poetry is the breaking down of the notion of simple truths, the literalness of the word, the notion of fixed commandments of behavior and morality sent down from heaven, the notion of an exclusive culture that can dominate another, the divine right of kings and the not so divine rights of the affluent and comfortable, the notion that God is with us and that these divine revelations we hold to be self-evident are equally true for others. The only absolutes for poetry are diversity and change (and the freedom to pursue these); and the only purpose, over the long run, is to raise questions, to raise doubts, to put people into alternative, sometimes uncomfortable situations, to raise questions but not necessarily answer them, or to jump ahead with other questions, to challenge the most widely held of preconceptions in our culture, that "Western man" is the culmination of the human evolutionary process.

INTERVIEWER: It's maddening, the way you raise questions but don't give answers.

ROTHENBERG: I wish I gave answers less, in fact. I'm appalled at what people do with answers or what answers do to people. And answers have consequences I don't like. They get fixed in the mind. I don't like to see fixed ends. I like to see the thwarting of ends.

Conducted April 9, 1979 by Zenia Cleigh, & later published in *San Diego Magazine*.

BIBLIOGRAPHY

Publications by Jerome Rothenberg

POEMS

White Sun Black Sun. New York: Hawk's Well Press, 1960.

The Seven Hells of the Jigoku Zoshi. New York: Trobar Books, 1962.

Sightings I–IX. New York: Hawk's Well Press, 1964.

The Gorky Poems. Mexico: El Corno Emplumado, 1966.

Between: Poems 1960–1963. London: Fulcrum Press, 1967.

Conversations. Los Angeles: Black Sparrow Press, 1968.

Sightings & Red Easy A Color (with prints by Ian Tyson). London: Circle Books, 1968.

Poems 1964–1967. Los Angeles: Black Sparrow Press, 1968.

Poland/1931 (first installment). Santa Barbara: Unicorn Press, 1969.

A Book of Testimony. San Francisco: Tree Books, 1971.

Poems for the Game of Silence. New York: Dial Press, 1971; reprinted, New York: New Directions, 1975.

Esther K. Comes to America (with cover by Eleanor Antin, photographs by Laurence Fink). Santa Barbara: Unicorn Press, 1973.

Seneca Journal 1: A Poem of Beavers. Mount Horeb, Wisconsin: Perishable Press, 1973.

Poland/1931 (complete). New York: New Directions, 1974.

The Cards. Los Angeles: Black Sparrow Press, 1974.

The Pirke & the Pearl. San Francisco: Tree Books, 1975.

Seneca Journal: Midwinter (box, with objects & collage by the author & Philip Sultz). St. Louis: Singing Bone Press, 1975.

A Poem to Celebrate the Spring & Diane Rothenberg's Birthday. Mount Horeb, Wisconsin: Perishable Press, 1975.

The Notebooks. Milwaukee: Membrane Press, 1976.

A Seneca Journal (complete). New York: New Directions, 1978.

Seneca Journal: The Serpent (with painted folders by Philip Sultz). St. Louis: Singing Bone Press, 1978.

Narratives & Realtheater Pieces (with woodcuts by Ian Tyson). Lot, France: Braad Editions, 1978.

Abulafia's Circles. Milwaukee: Membrane Press, 1979.

B*R*M*Tz*V*H. Mount Horeb, Wisconsin: Perishable Press, 1979.

Numbers & Letters. Madison, Wisconsin: Salient Seedling Press, 1980.

Vienna Blood. New York: New Directions, 1980.

TRANSLATIONS

New Young German Poets. San Francisco: City Lights Books, 1959.

The Deputy, by Rolf Hochhuth (American Playing Version). New York: Samuel French, 1965.

Poems for People Who Don't Read Poems, by Hans Magnus Enzensberger (co-translator with Enzensberger & Michael Hamburger). New York: Atheneum, 1968; London: Secker & Warburg, 1968.

The Flight of Quetzalcoatl (Aztec). Brighton, England: Unicorn Books, 1967.

The Book of Hours & Constellations, by Eugen Gomringer. New York: Something Else Press, 1968.

The 17 Horse Songs of Frank Mitchell (Navajo, with prints by Ian Tyson). London: Tetrad Press, 1970.

Gematria 27 (Hebrew, with Harris Lenowitz). Milwaukee: Membrane Press, 1977.

Songs for the Society of the Mystic Animals (Seneca, with typographical realizations by Ian Tyson). London: Tetrad Press, 1980.

ANTHOLOGIES

Ritual. New York: Something Else Press, 1966.

Technicians of the Sacred. New York: Doubleday-Anchor, 1967.

Shaking the Pumpkin. New York: Doubleday-Anchor, 1972.

America a Prophecy (with George Quasha). New York: Random House, 1973.

Revolution of the Word. New York: Seabury-Continuum, 1974.

Ethnopoetics: A First International Symposium (with Michel Benamou). Boston: Alcheringa & Boston University, 1976.

A Big Jewish Book (with Harris Lenowitz & Charles Doria). New York: Doubleday-Anchor, 1978.

Symposium of the Whole: An Ethnopoetics Reader (with Diane Rothenberg). Berkeley: University of California Press, scheduled 1981.

MAGAZINES

Poems from the Floating World. New York: 1960–1964; reprinted, New York: AMS Reprints, 1972.

Some/Thing (with David Antin). New York: 1965–1969; reprinted, New York: AMS Reprints, 1972.

Alcheringa (with Dennis Tedlock). New York & Boston: Boston University, 1970–1976.

New Wilderness Letter. New York: New Wilderness Foundation, 1976 to the present.

PRE-FACES & INTRODUCTIONS

Futz, & What Came After, by Rochelle Owens. New York: Random House, 1968.

Shango de Ima, by Pepe Carrill. New York: Doubleday, 1970.

Finding the Center, by Dennis Tedlock. New York: Dial Press, 1972.

Origins: Creation Texts from the Ancient Mediterranean, by Harris Lenowitz & Charles Doria. New York: Doubleday, 1976.

The Wishing Bone Cycle, by Howard Norman. New York: Stonehill Publishers, 1976.

The Florence Poems, by Toby Olson. London: Permanent Press, 1978.

Maria Sabina: Her Life & Chants, by Alvaro Estrada. Santa Barbara: Ross-Erikson Publishers, 1980.

Representative Works, by Jackson Mac Low. Santa Barbara: Ross-Erikson Publishers, 1981.

RECORDINGS

Origins & Meanings. New York: Folkways-Broadside, 1968.

From a Shaman's Notebook. New York: Folkways-Broadside, 1968.

Horse Songs & Other Soundings. Düsseldorf/Munich: S-Press Tonbandverlag, 1975.

6 Horse Songs for 4 Voices. New York: New Wilderness Audiographics, 1978.

Jerome Rothenberg Reads Poland/1931. Milwaukee: New Fire Cassette Series, 1979.

FOREIGN LANGUAGE EDITIONS

Poemas Gorky ("The Gorky Poems"), translated into Spanish by Sergio Mondragón & Margaret Randall. Mexico: El Corno Emplumado, 1966.

Dikter kring ett spel om tystnaden ("Poems for the Game of Silence"), translated into Swedish by Jan Ostergren. Sweden: Bo Cavefors Bokförlag, 1976.

Poèmes pour le jeu du silence ("Poems for the Game of Silence"), translated into French by Didier Pemerle, Jean Pierre Faye, & Jacques Roubaud. Paris: Editions Bourgois, 1978.

ACKNOWLEDGMENTS

The following material is reprinted in *Pre-Faces* with grateful acknowledgment to the editors and publishers of the books in which it first appeared: "New Models, New Visions: Some Notes Toward a Poetics of Performance" in Michael Benamou and Charles Caramello, *Performance in Postmodern Culture* (Coda Press, Copyright © 1977); "Pre-Face III," in Jerome Rothenberg, *Revolution of the Word: A New Gathering of Avant Garde Poetry* (Copyright © 1974 by Jerome Rothenberg; reprinted by permission of The Continuum Publishing Corporation); "Pre-Face V," "Gematria," "Abraham Abulafia," "At the Boundaries," "Sounding Events," "Tree Spirit Events," "Jesus," "Rain Event One," in Jerome Rothenberg, *A Big Jewish Book* (published by Anchor Press/Doubleday, 1978, Copyright © 1978 by Jerome Rothenberg; reprinted by permission of the Publisher); "Pre-Face II," "An Academic Proposal," "Gift Event," "The Raingod Drama," "Old Man Coyote," "Crazy Dog Events," in *Shaking the Pumpkin* (pubished by Doubeday/Anchor, 1972, Copyright © 1972 by Jerome Rothenberg; reprinted by permission of the Publisher); "Pre-Face I," "The Poetics of Sound," "Namings," "Images," "Bantu Combinations," "Praise Poems/Assemblages," "The Poetics of Chance (I): 'The Book of Changes,'" "The Poetics of Chance (II): 'The Praises of the Falls,'" "The Poetics of Shamanism," "God's Sexuality," "Offering Flowers," "The Ghost Dance," "The Night Chant," "Kunapipi," in Jerome Rothenberg, *Technicians of the Sacred* (published by Anchor Press/Doubleday, 1968, Copyright © 1968 by Jerome Rothenberg; reprinted by permission of the Publisher); "A Personal Manifesto," in Jerome Rothenberg, *Poems for the Game of Silence* (Copyright © 1966 by Jerome Rothenberg; reprinted by permission of New Directions). Excerpts are also used from Stanley Diamond, *In Search of the Primitive* (Copyright © 1974 by Transaction, Inc.; published by permission of Transaction, Inc.), and Marcea Eliade, *The Myth of Eternal Return, or, Cosmos and History,* trans. Willard R. Trask (Bollingen Series XLVI, Copyright 1954 by Princeton University Press; excerpts reprinted by permission).

INDEX

A (Zukofsky), 53
Abulafia, Abraham, 126, 160–61
The Acts of St. John, 51, 126, 200
"The Air of June" (Dorn), 54
"Alberto Rojas Jimenez Viene
  Volando" (Neruda), 204
Alcheringa, 15, 31n
Aldington, Richard, 107
"All Religions Are One" (Blake),
  57
"Alphabet Event," 21
alternative traditions, 27, 28–33, 44,
  112, 121
American Indians [frequently
  under tribal designations], 13, 15,
  18, 21, 30, 32, 36, 69, 71, 77, 93–98,
  99, 120n, 142, 143, 146, 170, 175,
  186, 187, 192, 197, 198–99, 203,
  208–10, 212–13, 214–15; translating
  Indian poetry, 76–92; & wilderness,
  176–85. *See also* oral poems
  quoted; Navajo; Seneca
*Ancient Near Eastern Texts
  Relating to the Old Testament*
  (Pritchard), 115
Anderson, Margaret, 108
"Anglo-Mongrels & the Rose" (Loy),
  109
anthologies, 3, 4, 139–43
*Anthology of New American &
  British Poets* (Hall-Pack-Simpson),
  103
Antin, David, 19, 20, 28, 33, 34, 46,
  52, 94, 101, 104, 105, 131, 140, 169
"Aphorisms on Futurism" (Loy),
  108
Apollinaire, Guillaume, 67, 104,
  107, 108
Arensberg, Walter Conrad, 108
Aristotle, 73, 156
"Asphodel, That Greeny Flower"
  (Williams), 195
Astrov, Margot, 175
Auden, W. H., 22, 102
avant-garde, 4, 5, 21, 26, 52, 100,
  101, 103–11. *See also* Modernism,
  Post-modernism
"Aztec Definitions," *see* Florentine
  Codex

Ball, Hugo, 140
Barth, John, 42
Baudelaire, Charles, 28

Beat poetry, Beat poets, 74, 103
Beckett, Samuel, 42
Beier, Ulli, 96, 152
Benamou, Michel, 129
Berg, Stephen, 97
Bérard, Victor, 115
Berndt, R. M. 96, 205–6
Berrigan, Ted, 104
Bible, 99, 113, 124, 126 (Revela-
  tion), 127, 164 (Samuel), 178,
  190–91 (Genesis). *See also* Torah
Bitahatini (the Visionary), 203
Blackburn, Paul, 18, 24, 35
Black Elk, 183, 203
Black Elk Speaks, 203
Black Mountain poets, 103, 111
Black Mountain Review, 103
Blake, William, 10, 12, 15, 17, 22,
  23, 32, 45, 51, 56–57, 58, 59, 60,
  65, 73, 74, 104, 110, 120n, 121, 139,
  152, 153, 190, 193
Blast, 108
Bleek, W. H. I., & Lloyd, L. C., 96
blues, 20, 99, 104, 192–93
Bly, Robert, 52, 54, 59, 63n
Boas, Franz, 96
Bodenheim, Maxwell, 108
Bohannan, Paul, 18
*Book of Circles/Life of the World
  to Come* (Abulafia), 160
Book of the Dead (Egyptian), 113
Book of Moses on the Secret Name,
  126
Bowra, C. M., 145
Brancusi, Constantine, 25
Breton, André, 14, 42, 63, 111, 120n
The Bridge (Crane), 109
Brooks, Cleanth, 33, 35
Brown, Bob, 103, 108
Buber, Martin, 57
Burchfield, Charles, 23
Burns, Robert, 30
Burroughs, William S., 55

Cage, John, 19, 21, 35, 46, 103, 111,
  167
Calas, Nicolas, 66, 75
Callaway, H., 187
Camera Work, 107, 108
Campbell, Joseph, 115
The Cantos (Pound), 27, 101, 108
Cary, Carl, 97
Cassirer, Ernst, 72

Catullus, 97
Celan, Paul, 63, 119
"Ceremonial Bundles of the Black-
  foot Indians" (Wissler), 187
chance, chance operations, 14, 15,
  21, 42, 43, 73 (random poetry), 103,
  152–55, 157; & divination, 152, 155
Chapman, John, 213
Chaucer, Geoffrey, 97
civilization (Western, etc.), 17, 18,
  28, 171, 184–85, 217, 224; as
  "European hegemony," 40. See also
  nation-state
"clash of symbols," 33, 117
clowns, sacred, 79, 208–10, 214
collage (assemblage), 3, 4, 40, 42,
  105–6, 109, 110, 111, 153, 155;
  anthologies as collage, 143; &
  African praise poems, 151–52
Concrete poetry, 15, 42, 43, 73, 96,
  103, 104, 106, 110, 167
Confucius, 153
Contact, 109
contradiction, conflict, 29, 31, 33,
  45, 46, 135, 219; in Ancient Near
  East, 117; among Aztecs, 150–51;
  as dialectic, 45; & image, 148–49;
  in Jewish tradition, 121, 124; &
  monoculture, 223; in "primitive"
  poetry, 72, 73; & raising doubt, 75,
  223–24. See also opposites, "clash
  of symbols"
Cordovero, Moses, 126
El Corno Emplumado, 80
Corso, Gregory, 55
Cosmos and History (Eliade), 25
Crane, Hart, 102, 105, 109
"Crazy Dog Events," 214–15
Creeley, Robert, 28, 33, 52–64 (cor-
  respondence with), 62 ("The
  Door")
Crosby, Harry, 104, 109, 111 (&
  Caresse Crosby)
Cubism, 41; Cubist poetry, 46, 107,
  111
Cummings, E. E., 24, 99, 103, 104,
  108

Dada, Dadaists, 14, 21, 24, 74, 99,
  142, 214; New York Dada, 108; &
  performance, 165–66
Dali, Salvador, 99
Dante Alighieri, 28, 29, 30, 195
Dasmann, Ray, 179
A Day Book (Creeley), 33
Dead Sea Scrolls, 126
deep image, 52–64, 73, 104, 139, 153;
  distinguished from "pictorial im-
  age," 53, 55, 56, 59; as "sparks"
  [kabbala], 57; & speaking/writing,

53, 60–61, 62; & Surrealism, 60; &
  verse line or form, 54, 58–59,
  61–62; & visionary poetry, 56–59,
  61–62. See also image, imagina-
  tion, vision
Densmore, Frances, 96, 99
Derrida, Jacques, 143
De Soto, Hernando, 192
De Stijl (movement), 104
Diamond, Stanley, 18, 29, 41, 76,
  120, 133, 183, 194
Dickinson, Emily, 32, 34, 102
dilug (skipping), 161
Disney, Walt, 177
Djanggawul, 147
Donne, John, 28, 29
"The Door" (Creeley), 62
Doria, Charles, 31, 112, 116–17
Dorn, Edward, 54
Dostoyevsky, Feodor, 25, 213
dream, 14, 42, 73, 74, 109, 118, 127,
  166, 187, 208; dream-time, 39, 110,
  120; dream-work, 167
Duchamp, Marcel, 17, 24, 103, 105,
  108, 109, 171
Dunbar, William, 61n
Duncan, Robert, 16, 28, 52, 54–55,
  59, 61, 62, 104, 111, 115, 119, 171

Earth House Hold (Snyder), 33
Economou, George, 52
Edmonson, Munro, 97
Ein Sof ("the limitless"), 162
Eisagoge ("Tragedy of Moses"),
  126–27
Eliade, Mircea, 25, 38–39, 43, 65,
  70n, 115, 186, 187, 188
Eliot, T. S., 13, 22, 23, 24, 25, 27,
  28, 32, 33, 39, 41, 100–1, 108, 109
Emerson, Ralph Waldo, 32, 63
Empedocles, 117
Enoch, Book of, 126
Enuma Elish (Babylonian), 31, 113
Epic of Gilgamesh, 31, 113, 184–85
Epstein, Jacob, 25
Eshleman, Clayton, 52, 204
ethnopoetics, ethnos, 15, 19, 43,
  129–36 ("Pre-Face to a Symposium
  on . . ."), 135, 143; model of per-
  formance in, 131
Euripedes, 117
Experimental Review, 111
Ezekielos, 127
Ezra, Fourth Book of, 126

Fearing, Kenneth, 110
Field, Edward, 97
The Fifties [Sixties, etc.], 62, 62n
Finkelstein, Louis, 124
Finlay, Ian Hamilton, 148

First International Symposium on Ethnopoetics, 129

Florentine Codex (Sahagún), 118 (quoted), 149–51, 184 (quoted), 194 (also called "Aztec Definitions")

Ford, Charles Henri, 110

For Love (Creeley), 33

Four Saints in Three Acts (Stein), 46

Francis of Assisi, 194

Frank, Jacob, (Frankists), 125, 126

freedom/liberation (in the poem, etc.), 5, 58–59, 101, 104, 106, 120, 135, 151, 157, 200; & "nihilist mystics," 121–22

Freud, Sigmund, 40, 167

von Freytag-Loringhoven, Else, 108, 109

Frost, Robert, 63, 102

Fuller, Buckminster, 13, 14

Futurists, Futurism, 21, 107, 142

Gaudier-Brzeska, Henri, 25

Gbadamosi, Bakare, 152

gematria, 156, 158–59. *See also* number, poetry of

A General History of the Things of New Spain (Sahagún), 194. *See* Florentine Codex

Genet, Jean, 42

Ghost Dance, 198–99

"Gift Event" (Kwakiutl), 197

Gillespie, Abraham Lincoln, 110

Ginsberg, Allen, 28, 33, 54, 104, 127

"Giveaway Construction" (Knowles), 197

Gnosticism, gnosis, 114, 117, 121, 122, 125, 126, 162, 200

goddess, 30, 103, 109, 192–93, 204 (Kunapipi), 208. *See also* Shekinah

"god names" (Egyptian), 145

Grant, Michael, 124

Graves, Robert, 115, 196

Great Subculture, 17, 31, 52, 103, 107, 115–16 (defined by Gary Snyder), 121, 134, 196. *See also* alternative traditions

Great Tradition, 4, 23, 28; "greater tradition," 28–33; 165–66. *See also* alternative traditions, Great Subculture

Greek Anthology, 175

Haile, Father Berard, 144

Hall, Donald, 103

happenings, 74, 96, 128, 166, 169, 197

Hartley, Marsden, 108

Hasidic Prayer (Jacobs), 164

Hawthorne, Nathaniel, 32

Heap, Jane, 108

The Hebrew Goddess (Patai), 211

H. D. (Hilda Doolittle), 107

Heidegger, Martin, 9, 12

Heisenberg, Werner, 13

Hesiod, 114, 117

Hillel the Elder, 196

Hillman, James, 141

Hirschman, Jack, 119, 161

history, 19, 31, 38–39, 39–41, 46, 105–6, 120, 122, 132–33, 140; relation to poetic past, 135–36, 140, 219

Hollo, Anselm, 97

Homer, 31, 45, 112, 113, 114, 117, 175

"Horse Songs," 21, 76, 77–78, 85–91, 97, 140, 142 (translation quoted)

Huidobro, Vicente, 59

"Human Universe" (Olson), 10

Hymes, Dell, 76, 77

"I Ain't Got Nobody" (B. White), 193

"I Am Under L.A. International Airport" (S. Ortiz), 185

I Ching ("The Book of Changes"), 152–54, 155

image, poetic, 46, 60, 141, 146–48; contrasted to symbol, 42; image combinations, 148–49; image-thinking, 73, 152–53; Ezra Pound on, 105; Pierre Reverdy on, 149, 159; as riddle, 148; & song, 147; & translation, 63, 159. *See also* deep image, imagination

imagination, 45, 59, 60, 69; dialectical imagination, 168; "new" imagination, 58, 60

Imagists, Imagism, 25, 44, 45–46, 55, 60, 107, 108, 110

intermedia, 106, 128, 167; in American Indian Poetry, 95, 202; "primitive" & avant-garde, 21, 74, 96

In the American Grain (Williams), 32, 192

Inyo-Kutavere, 170

Ionesco, Eugene, 42

Isaiah, 31

Ishmael ben Elisha, 126

Isou, Isidore, 161

Jabès, Edmond, 119, 123, 165

Jacobs, Louis, 164

Jakobson, Roman, 34

Jarrell, Randall, 22, 103

Jefferson, Thomas, 14, 65

Jesus, 51, 124, 126, 198, 200–1
Jewish Magic & Superstition
 (Trachtenberg), 160
Jews, 16, 31, 118–28, 143; & Ancient
 Near East, Greeks, etc., 31, 112–17;
 & Jesus, 200–1; & language, 123,
 124, 143, 162; as "mental rebels,"
 123, 161; & poetry (poesis), 121–23,
 127, 196; as rainmakers, 211. *See
 also* number, poetry of
The Jews in the Roman World
 (Grant), 124
*The Jews: Their History, Culture,
 & Religion* (Finkelstein), 124
Jimerson, Avery, 81–82, 169
Jimerson, Fidelia, 81–82
John, Floyd, 169
Johnny John, Richard, 79, 80–81,
 83, 129, 130
Jolas, Eugene, 110
Jones, LeRoi [Amiri Baraka], 93
Joyce, James, 25, 44 (quoted *qua*
 Stephen Dedalus), 99, 108, 110, 115
Jung, Carl, 60, 153, 212
Junod, Henri, 148–49
Justin's *Baruch*, 117

kabbala, kabbalists, 16, 18, 21, 117,
 121, 125, 126, 127, 158–62, 200;
 deep image & kabbalistic sparks,
 57
Kaddish (Ginsberg), 33, 54
Kafka, Franz, 42, 119, 125, 147
Kaprow, Allan, 128, 167
Keats, John, 10, 141
Kelly, Robert, 52, 53–54, 56, 58, 59,
 61, 96, 115
Knowles, Alison, 197
Koller, James, 97
Kramer, Samuel Noah, 115
Kreymborg, Alfred, 108
Kroeber, Alfred L., 170
Kunapipi (Berndt), 205–7

Laforgue, Jules, 28
Lamantia, Philip, 111
Lame Deer, 183
"Lament for the Makers" (Dunbar),
 61n
language, 34, 42, 106, 109, 112–13,
 137, 143; comic & god language,
 208–9; in Jewish tradition, 123;
 "primitive" languages, 69; &
 revolution, 66–67
Lanier, Sydney, 102
Laski, Vera, 209, 210
Lautréamont, Comte de, (Isidore
 Ducasse), 110

Lawrence, D. H., 25, 27, 63
Leavis, F. R., 33
Lenowitz, Harris, 31, 112, 116–17
Lectures in America (Stein), 145–46
Leon, Moses de, 126
Levertov, Denise, 52
Lévi-Strauss, Claude, 30, 34, 120n,
 177
Lewis, Wyndham, 25, 108
The Little Review, 108, 109
The Living Desert (Disney), 177
Living Theater, 128
Lorca, Federico García, 59, 63, 74,
 99
Lowell, Amy, 107
Lowell, Robert, 22, 103
Lowenfels, Walter, 78, 103, 110, 111
Lowie, Robert, 97, 212, 215
Loy, Mina, 103, 108, 109
Luria, Isaac, 126

Mac Low, Jackson, 21, 46, 103, 111,
 127, 128, 134, 158, 161, 169
Malinowski, Bronislaw, 43, 144, 154
Mallarmé, Stephen, 41
Mapetla, Joas, 154
Marpa, 97
Marshack, Alexander, 30
Marx, Karl, 40, 66, 125
"Masturbation Genesis" (Egyptian),
 190
Matthews, Washington, 96, 202–3
Maximus Poems (Olson), 15, 33, 55
Mayer, Bernadette, 20
McAllester, David, 76, 77, 85–90, 96,
 97
McAlmon, Robert, 109
McLuhan, Marshall, 11, 73
Meltzer, David, 119
Melville, Herman, 32
Merwin, W. S., 96, 97
The Messianic Idea in Judaism
 (Scholem), 200–1
Metaphysical poets, poetry, 28, 29,
 33
Metraux, Alfred, 187
Milton, John, 32, 190
minimal poetry (traditional), 73–74,
 79, 83
Mishna, 121, 127
Mitchell, Frank, 76, 77, 86–91
Modernism, 22–25, 44, 45, 46,
 99–111, 120; & "middle ground,"
 99, 109; & the "primitive," 20,
 26–28; & traditional models,
 165–66; & visionary poetry, 99, 109.
 See also avant-garde, Post-
 modernism
Modigliani, Amedeo, 25
Mondragón, Sergio, 80

monoculture, 121, 221 (& localism), 223
Moon-Bone Cycle, 147
Mooney, James, 199
Moore, Marianne, 24
Mottram, Eric, 157
Mureau (Cage), 21
Mythologies of the Ancient World, (Kramer), 115

naming, 122, 126, 145–46, 153; Egyptian "god names," 145; The Path of Names, 160; praise-names, 151
Narration (Stein), 139
nation-state, 12, 68, 96, 120, 135, 157, 161, 168, 223; & Fascism, 27. *See also* civilization
Navajo Indians, 144, 182. *See also* "Horse Songs"; Night Chant
The Navajo Night Chant (Matthews), 202
Neihardt, John, 203
Neruda, Pablo, 63, 203–4
New Criticism, 22, 24, 25, 28, 33–35, 36, 38, 42, 100, 104
New Wilderness Letter, 31n
New York school (poets), 103
Night Chant (Navajo), 202–4
Nixon, Richard M., 10
"Notes on the Poetry of Image" (Kelly), 52, 53–54, 56, 58
Notes from Underground (Dostoyevsky), 25
number, poetry of, 156–57, 196. *See also* gematria

"Objectivists," "Objectivism," 13, 14, 24, 42, 103, 110–11
An "Objectivists" Anthology (Zukofsky), 110–11
"Ocean Stripe Series" (Finlay), 148
O'Hara, Frank, 55, 103
Oliveros, Pauline, 28
Olson, Charles, 10, 12, 13, 15, 17, 24, 28, 31, 33, 34, 36, 40, 43, 55, 57, 103, 111, 112, 115, 121, 170
Oppen, George, 13, 105, 110, 111
opposites, tension of, 212; union as "implosion," 210. *See also* contradiction
oral poems quoted (anonymous): Apache, 182; Australian Aborigine, 71, 142, 144, 206–7; Bantu, 148–49; Basuto, 154; Bushman, 71, 146; Crow, 181; Eskimo, 146, 180; Huichol, 185; Lummi, 181; Navajo, 182, 202; Ojibwa (Chippewa), 71, 182; Seneca, 81–82, 83–84, 129–30, 181; Seri, 181;

Sioux, 181; Thompson River, 182; Yoruba, 151. *See also* "Horse Songs," "Shaking the Pumpkin" (ceremony)
oral poetry, 9–47; "new oral poetry," 36; oral & literal, 13, 14, 15, 16, 19, 135, 161; Oral Torah, 16, 200; oral tradition, 15–18, 20, 120, 126, 130; & translation, 76–92; & visionary poetry, 44–46, 60–61, 62; & writing, 10–12, 36, 121, 130, 131; vocables & wordless poems in, 20, 70, 71, 74, 77–78, 82, 95, 140, 144–45. *See also* sound poetry
Origin, 103
Origins (Lenowitz & Doria), 31, 112–17 (Pre–Face)
Ortiz, Alfonso, 182–83, 208
Ortiz, Simon, 185, 213
"Osage Simultaneities," 21
Others, 108
Ovid, 117
Owens, Rochelle, 96, 119

Pack, Robert, 103
Paleolithic (Stone Age), 30–31, 33, 103, 115–16, 120, 133, 134
"Paradiso" (Dante), 30
Parrish, Essie, 183
Patai, Raphael, 211
Patchen, Kenneth, 103, 110
Paterson (Williams), 19
performance, poetics of, 3, 5, 20–21, 34, 35, 74, 106, 129–36, 165–71; & audience, 169–70; in "primitive" poetry, 70, 72, 129; & shamans, 133–35; as "sounding," 35, 36, 37, 130–31, 132, 163–64 (*see also* oral poetry; sound poetry); of stand-up poet, 21, 131–32; contrasted to "understanding," 35–36. *See also* ritual
Picabia, Francis, 108
Picasso, Pablo, 25
Pieces (Creeley), 33
Pinter, Harold, 42
"The Plan" (Creeley), 53
Plato, 12
Poe, Edgar Allan, 102, 193
"Poem Beginning with a Line by Pindar" (Duncan), 54–55
Poèmes nègres (Tzara), 165–66
Poems from the Floating World, 3, 56, 56n, 62, 64, 139
poesis, 116, 118, 120, 121–23
poet, as seer, 13, 15, 74, 105, 121, 186; eye-orientation (I & eye), 12–15, 44, 45. *See also* shamanism, visionary poetry
Poetry, and animals, 74, 106, 166,

167, 179–81; & body, 74; of
changes, 16, 25, 28–29, 44, 47,
106, 136, 217, 219, 223; in the
classroom, 36–38, 175; of corre-
spondences, 153, 158; function in,
18, 34–35, 37, 135, 169–70; of
hunters, 180–84; & mysticism, 158,
121–22, 160, 222–23 (*see also*
kabbala); of permutations, 160; &
sexuality, 74, 115, 190–91. *See also*
chance operations; Concrete
poetry; naming; number, poetry
of; oral poetry; performance,
poetics of; poesis; poet as seer;
"primitive" poetry; signing
poetry; sound poetry; visionary
poetry
Poetry, 107, 111
Pope, Alexander, 223
Popol Vuh, 97, 175
Porcupine, 198
Porges, Moses, 122
Porter, Bern, 111
Post-modernism, 9, 22, 41–42, 45,
46
Pound, Ezra, 13, 14, 23, 24, 25, 27,
31, 40, 41, 46, 63, 64, 96, 97, 99,
101, 102, 103, 105, 106, 107–8, 110,
115, 121
Powhattan, 93
praise poems, 147, 151–52, 154–55
The "primitive" (tribal/oral cul-
tures), 16, 17–18, 22, 25, 26–28, 29,
36, 43, 129, 133 (hunters &
gatherers), 220; alternative terms
for, 69n, 76; faced with extinc-
tion, 18, 220–21; "primitive means
complex," 69–71. *See also* "primi-
tive" poetry
"primitive" (tribal/oral) poetry, 5,
69–75, 76, 95, 96, 103, 144, 165–66;
collective nature of, 70; compared
to contemporary, 20–21, 38, 52,
73–75, 129, 153, 166n–67n, 219; &
performance, 70, 72, 129; "primi-
tive poem" defined, 71–73; song
practice in, 147. *See also* the
"primitive"; oral poetry
Primitive Song (Bowra), 145
Pritchard, James B., 115
"Projective Verse" (Olson), 24, 57,
103, 153
Pynchon, Thomas, 42

Quain, Buell, 96
Quasha, George, 28, 38

Radin, Paul, 95, 133, 194
"Rain Event One," 211

Raingod Drama (San Juan Pueblo),
208–10
Rakosi, Carl, 110
Randall, Margaret, 80
Ransom, John Crowe, 22, 102
Rasmussen, Knud, 97, 186
Ray, Man, 108
Religion of the Crow (Lowie), 212
*The Religious System of the
Amazulu* (Callaway), 187
repetition & redundancy, 20, 21, 147
"Revelation & Tradition as Re-
ligious Categories" (Scholem), 16
Reverdy, Pierre, 149
revolution, & poets, poetry, 65–68,
106, 110; the "poet/rebel," 161; in
"taste," 101; in technology, 104–5;
"of the word," 103, 106, 110. *See
also* freedom; nation-state
"Revolutions & Revolutionaries in
Literature" (symposium), 67–68
Rexroth, Kenneth, 102, 103, 111
Reznikoff, Charles, 110
Ricoeur, Paul, 31, 117
Rilke, Rainer Maria, 74
Rimbaud, Arthur, 13, 30, 32, 74,
110, 120n, 121, 186, 188
ritual, 35, 74, 96, 147, 150, 183,
202–3 (Night Chant), 205–6
(Kunapipi), 208–10 (Pueblo
drama); & contemporary perfor-
mance, 166n–67n, 207. *See also*
performance, poetics of
Robinson, Edwin Arlington, 102
Roethke, Theodore, 103
Rogue, 108
Romantics, Romanticism, 17, 32,
133
Rothenberg, Jerome, *America a
Prophecy*, 22, 32, 33, 38, 140; *A
Big Jewish Book*, 118–28 (Pre-
Face), 143, 156; *Poland/1931*, 21,
33, 43, 119, 140, 143; *Revolution
of the Word*, 32, 99–111 (Pre-
Face), 143; *A Seneca Journal*, 43,
169; *Shaking the Pumpkin*, 11,
20, 21, 33, 85, 93–98 (Pre-Face),
143; "Sightings," 141; *6 Horse
Songs for 4 Voices*, 91n; *Techni-
cians of the Sacred*, 3–4, 5, 11, 20,
33, 36, 43, 69–75 (Pre-Face), 76,
96, 119, 122, 127, 141, 143, 166n,
175; *White Sun Black Sun*, 52, 54n
("Invincible Flowers"), 55. *See
also Alcheringa*, "Horse Songs,"
*New Wilderness Letter, Poems
from the Floating World*
"Round Dance of Jesus," 126
Rukeyser, Muriel, 110

234

Sabbatai, Zevi, (Sabbateans), 125, 126, 200–1
de Sahagún, Bernardino, 149–51, 194
Sanders, Ed, 96
Sartre, Jean-Paul, 42
Satie, Éric, 21
Schechner, Richard, 167, 169, 183
Scholem, Gershom, 16, 121–22, 162, 200–1
Scholes, Robert, 36
Schuyler, James, 103
Schwartz, Delmore, 23, 100, 101, 102, 103
Schwerner, Armand, 52, 59, 97, 115, 212
Schwitters, Kurt, 140
Seami Motokiyo, 194
Sefer ha-Hekhalot ("The Book of Palaces"), 126
Sefer ha-Razim ("The Book of Mysteries"), 126
Sejourné, Laurette, 194
Seneca Indians, 36, 76, 77, 94, 129–30, 134, 169, 181; translating Seneca poetry, 78–85
Shakespeare, William, 99
"Shaking the Pumpkin" (ceremony), 82–85, 129–131 (also called *Idos*, Society of the Mystic Animals)
shamanism, shamans, 12, 13, 30, 33, 43, 74, 117, 120–21, 124, 166, 179–80, 183, 186–89, 202; defined, 186; as prototype of poet, 105, 133–35, 186; as "technicians of the sacred," 70n, 120; & song, 186–88
Shamanism (Eliade), 187, 188
"Le Shamanisme chez les Indiens de l'Amerique du Sud Tropicale" (Metraux), 187
Shekinah, 121, 122, 164, 193. See *also* goddess
A Shropshire Lad, 101
signing poetry, 44n (deaf), 142 (Indian)
Simeon bar Yohai, 126
Simon Magus, 126
Simpson, Louis, 103
Smart, Christopher, 56
Smith, Capt. John, 93
Smohalla, 179
Snodgrass, W. D., 101
Snyder, Gary, 18, 28, 33, 34, 52, 59, 76, 103, 115–16, 121, 127, 131, 170, 171, 179, 180, 189, 199
Solzhenitsyn, Aleksandr, 38
"Sounding Events," 163
sound poetry, 20–21, 42, 74, 77, 96, 99, 140, 142, 145; in kabbala, 128; sounds in Pueblo drama, 209; translation as Concrete poetry, 83–85; translation as sound, 85–91. See *also* oral poetry, vocables & wordless poems in; performance as "sounding"
Southern Fugitives, 102, 111 (as Nashville Critics). See *also* New Criticism
Spanos, William, 4, 9–47 (as interviewer)
Spenser, Edmund, 190
Stein, Gertrude, 19, 20, 24, 30, 34, 46, 99, 103, 105, 107, 108, 110, 125, 127, 139, 145–46, 153
Stevens, Wallace, 63, 108
Stieglitz, Alfred, 107
Structuralism in Literature: An Introduction (Scholes), 36
Surrealists, Surrealism, 14, 24, 27, 32, 40, 42, 55, 59, 73, 99, 104, 109, 110, 111, 119, 167; Surrealist image, 42
Symbolists, Symbolism, 25, 26, 41, 44, 45–46, 73, 111; symbol & image, 29–30; Symbolism & Post-symbolism, 42–43, 45–47
synchronicity, 38, 40, 105–6, 153

The Tablets (Schwerner), 115
Talking (Antin), 33
Talmud, 127, 164, 211. See *also Mishna*
Tarn, Nathaniel, 97, 120
Tate, Allen, 22, 23, 102, 109
Taylor, Edward, 32
Tedlock, Dennis, 15, 20, 97
Tender Buttons (Stein), 107
Tens, Isaac, 186, 203
"Thank You: A Poem in 17 Parts" (Johnny John), 80
"There Is No Natural Religion" (Blake), 57
Thoreau, Henry David, 32
Toldot Yeshu, 126
Torah, 16, 121n, 200, 201. See *also* Bible
Trachtenberg, Joshua, 160
transcendentalists, 32
Transition, 104, 110
translation, 3, 20, 21, 27, 62–64, 70, 76–92, 93–94, 96–97, 115–17, 159; as composition, 131, 142; & music, 87–88, 90–91; of songs as Concrete poetry, 83–85; "total translation," 76–92, 97; & vocables, 77–78, 83–85, 85–91

"Tree Spirit Events" (*Zohar*), 196
trickster, 29, 200, 212–13 (Coyote)
Trotsky, Leon, 125
tseruf (combination of letters), 160
Tsvetayeva, Marina, 123
Tu Fu, 26
Turner, Victor, 167, 168
291, 108
Tyler, Parker, 110
Tzara, Tristan, 24, 96, 125, 140,
    142, 165–66

Ulikummi (Hittite), 112, 113
Ulysses (Joyce), 108
Understanding Poetry (Brooks &
    Warren), 33, 35

Vergil, 117
Vexations (Satie), 21
View, 111
vision, visionary poetry, 13, 14, 15,
    17, 33, 39, 42, 43, 44, 120, 126, 134,
    149, 167; & deep image, 56–59;
    "envisioning," 30, 45; in Modern-
    ism, 99, 105, 109–10; & oral poetry/
    sounding, 44–46, 132; poetic/
    visionary continuum, 125; & song,
    186–89, 199, 203. *See also* poet as
    seer; shamanism
"Vocabularies" (Mac Low), 158
Vorticism, vortex, 105, 107, 108, 110
VVV, 104, 111

Wakoski, Diane, 52
Waley, Arthur, 96
Wallis, Wilson D., 194
Walum Olum (Delaware), 184
"The War of the Sons of Light
    Against the Sons of Darkness,"
    126
Warren, Robert Penn, 33, 35

The Waste Land (Eliot), 23, 101,
    109
"We have had our gene-" (Black-
    burn), 24
Weiner, Hannah, 142
White, Bukka, 192–93
The White Goddess (Graves), 103,
    196
Whitman, Walt, 12, 17, 19, 22, 23,
    32, 46, 58, 63, 102, 104, 106, 107,
    119
Wilbur, Richard, 103
wilderness, & eco-system, 179; &
    French *désert*, etc., 177–78; &
    Indians, 176–185; "new wilder-
    ness," 185
Wilhelm, Richard, 153
Williams, Jonathan, 103
Williams, William Carlos, 14, 19,
    23, 24, 46, 53, 55, 64, 96, 101, 102,
    103, 107, 108, 109, 110, 127, 192,
    195
Winged Serpent (Astrov), 175
Winters, Yvor, 102
Wissler, Clark, 187, 188
"The Woman" (Creeley), 53
Wood, Grant, 23
"Woman's Dance Songs" (Jimer-
    son), 81–82
Wordsworth, William, 176
Wovoka (Jack Wilson), 198–99

Yeats, William Butler, 22, 25, 41,
    58, 60, 102, 108
Yellow-brow, 214
Yohanan ben Zakkai, 164

Zohar, 121n, 126, 127, 156, 191, 196
Zukofsky, Louis, 13, 43, 53, 62, 84,
    103, 110–11, 127